PALACE OF BOOKS

Roger Grenier

TRANSLATED AND WITH A FOREWORD
BY ALICE KAPLAN

PALACE
of
BOOKS

The University of Chicago Press
Chicago and London

ROGER GRENIER, an editor at Éditions Gallimard, has published over thirty works of fiction and nonfiction, including *The Difficulty of Being a Dog* and *A Box of Photographs*, and is the recipient of numerous prizes, including the Grand Prix de Littérature de l'Académie Française.

ALICE KAPLAN is the author of *French Lessons*, *The Collaborator*, *The Interpreter*, and *Dreaming in French*. She has translated a number of books, including Roger Grenier's *The Difficulty of Being a Dog* and *A Box of Photographs*. She holds the John M. Musser chair in French literature at Yale. She lives in Guilford, Connecticut.

The University of Chicago Press, Chicago 60637
The University of Chicago Press, Ltd., London
© 2014 by The University of Chicago
All rights reserved. Published 2014.
Printed in the United States of America

23 22 21 20 19 18 17 16 15 14   1 2 3 4 5

ISBN-13: 978-0-226-30834-0 (cloth)
ISBN-13: 978-0-226-23259-1 (e-book)
DOI: 10.7208/chicago/9780226232591.001.0001

Originally published as *Le palais des livres*, © Éditions Gallimard, 2011.

Cet ouvrage a bénéficié du soutien des Programmes d'aide à la publication de l'Institut Français. This work, published as part of a program of aid for publication, received support from the Institut Français.

Library of Congress Cataloging-in-Publication Data

Grenier, Roger, 1919– author.
[Palais des livres. English]
Palace of books / Roger Grenier ; translated
and with a foreword by Alice Kaplan.
pages cm
Includes bibliographical references.
ISBN 978-0-226-30834-0 (cloth : alk. paper)
1. Essays—Authorship. 2. French literature—History and criticism.
I. Kaplan, Alice Yaeger. II. Title.
PQ2613.R4323P3513 2014
844'.914—dc23
2014015683

CONTENTS

FOREWORD

Alice Kaplan

Here is a "palace of books" where Proust, Flaubert, Nabokov, Flannery O'Connor, Chekhov, Baudelaire, Kafka wander happily alongside the author's own friends and colleagues — Romain Gary, Jean-Paul Sartre, Claude Roy — and his mentor, Albert Camus. Roger Grenier, who as an editor and author has shaped the face of literature in France for nearly five decades, has a critical method that might best be described as "phenomenology plus charm": he looks to literature, to writers, to elucidate life's mysteries. Why do people feel the need to write? Why is the act of waiting so central a theme in literature? Can writers know when they've written their last sentence, or is it always someone else who makes the call? What is the difference between putting your deepest self in a literary text and revealing your private life?

His book consists of nine essays: "'The Land of Poets'"; "Waiting and Eternity"; "Leave-Taking"; "Private Life"; "Writing about Love, Again . . ."; "A Half Hour at the Dentist's"; "Unfinished"; "Do I Have Anything Left to Say?"; and "To Be Loved." Each essay begins with a problem or theme and explores it through a form of argument disguised as literary free association. Grenier interrogates his favorite writers and wrests wisdom and humor from their novels and essays. On writing about love, for example, he reminds us that Chekhov worried that a story without women was like a steam engine without steam; that Alexandre Dumas and his collaborator were horrified when they realized they had gotten to the fortieth chapter of their sequel to *The Three Musketeers* without a single love story; that Camus's *The Plague* is the only major contemporary novel without major women characters, because Camus wanted to explore the horrors of separation in wartime. Grenier points out that Madame de Lafayette, in *The Princess of Cleves* (the first novel in the French canon), keeps saying how dangerous love is, and how it must be avoided. But she speaks of nothing else.

Readers of Grenier's *The Difficulty of Being a Dog* and *A Box of Photographs* will recognize his appeal. Never didactic, never pedantic, Grenier takes us by the hand gently, and without really realizing what is happening, we come away enlightened. *Palace of Books* answers a real need and demand for nonacademic criticism, and for what Francine Prose has called, in the American context, the pleasures of "reading like a writer."

PALACE OF BOOKS

"THE LAND OF POETS"[1]

Committing a crime means taking action. But accounting for a crime in the newspaper or on radio and television means transforming that action into a story, into words.

This creates problems. The public that feasts on crime needs its stories to have a beginning, a middle, and an end. It needs a small novel, more exciting than fiction because it's true. Reality rarely unfolds with such pleasing logic. It's usually impossible to know exactly when the slowly unfolding drama began, and just as impossible to make any sense of what the victims and protagonists had to say. The confusion isn't due to the facts but to something like a layer of concrete covering every motive, every attitude. Never has the Shakespearean-Faulknerian cliché about the "tale told by an idiot, full of sound and fury" been more apropos. This doesn't prevent reporters from inventing fine, well-crafted

1. From Stendhal: "Italy is the 'land of poets.'" *Translator's note*: We've used existing translations whenever available and occasionally adapted or edited them for accuracy. When Grenier refers to the title of a work for which no translation exists, the title is given in the original French, with an English translation in brackets. Full bibliographic references to works from which the author quotes and that are available in English can be found in Works Cited at the end of the book.

accounts that respond to the five basic Ws: Who, What, When, Where, Why.

Which is exactly what Freud did with Oedipus's crime. He simplified an awfully confusing story, giving it his own structure. Actually, if you back up a little, his Laius had a pretty unsavory past. He'd been banished from Thebes and had to seek asylum in Pisa and in Ilia, with Pelops. And when he was allowed to return, he brought Pelops's bastard son Chrysippus with him. Laius, gay? According to some accounts, he was the original pederast.

The Thebans commemorated him with a military regiment composed of adolescent boys and their lovers and known as the Sacred Band of Thebes. Chrysippus supposedly tried to kill himself in shame. But Pelops's wife, Hippodameia, is also rumored to have gone to Thebes to kill him. Why? Something about an inheritance. She tried to get Atreus and Thyestes, the two legitimate sons she'd had with Pelops, to murder both Laius and Chrysippus. Apparently they refused. One night she crept into the room where Laius lay in bed with a boy and plunged a sword into his heart. Laius was accused of the murder. Happily for him, Chrysippus was able to name the guilty party with his last breath. But not so fast. It's possible too that Atreus was involved in the crime, since he was in such a hurry to take asylum in Mycenae. As for Pelops, didn't people say he won his throne and Hippodameia's hand by winning a chariot race against Oenomaus, the princess's father, thanks to a winged chariot that—hold onto your seat—was apparently a present from his lover Poseidon? And Jocasta? Who knew that as priestess of Hera the Strangler she had a problem with Menoeceus, her father, one of the men sprung from the ground after Cadmus sowed the dragon's teeth. Like seed. Old Menoeceus thought that he was the one who designated Tiresias the prophet—not Oedipus. And he sacrificed himself by jumping off the wall of Thebes. (Oedipus also sprang from one of these dragon's teeth, in the third generation.) And why then did Odysseus call on Jocasta during his visit to the underworld? Homer gives Jocasta another name: Epicaste. This same Epicaste, Clymenus's wife, was also involved in an incest drama. Clymenus slept with their daughter Harpalyce, who then gave birth to a boy. Harpalyce killed her son, who was also her brother, and served him up to Clymenus on a platter.

I could go on and on. For the last few paragraphs, though, it's hard to make heads or tails of any of it. Where does the crime story begin? In what confusing past does it take root? How do you untangle so many contradictions when your assignment is to deliver a story that's all wrapped up and obeys the basic rules of causation?

I once heard about an old-fashioned newspaper editor who kept a set of questions and a standard outline to fit every situation. He had them for crimes, for fires, for derailed trains. Pity the reporter who returned to the paper without all the answers. He'd be sent right back to the far-flung suburb where he'd forgotten to note the age of the concierge.

These newspaper articles, with their accounts of crimes and accidents, work the same way literature does. The writer who tells a well-rounded story makes order in the world. Paul Valéry insisted that it is impossible to account for the precise time of a crime: "The crime cannot be located at the exact moment when the crime takes place, nor right before—but rather in a well-established situation, distant from the act, developed over time—the fruit of some inconsequential fantasy, or of the need to satisfy a passing impulse, or as a cure for boredom—often a result of considering all possible solutions without discriminating among them."

Valéry also writes: "Every crime has something dreamlike about it. A crime that is bound to take place engenders everything it needs: victims, circumstances, motives, opportunities."

Literature, pretensions aside, is reductive. The tragedy of Oedipus told by Sophocles and used by Freud is much like a news story. It begins with the most striking element, with what journalists call the "hook": The city of Thebes, beset by the plague, begs Oedipus to come to its rescue.

From the Greek myth to today's disaster tale, the gist of the *fait divers*—that untranslatable French expression meaning a news item about a crime, a scandal, a disaster, or some random act—hasn't changed. What has changed are the forms it takes. The New Yorker Weegee, photographing murdered gangsters lying on the sidewalks of Brooklyn or the Bronx night after night, offers us striking fixed images in a painterly chiaroscuro. He thought nothing of comparing himself to Rembrandt!

The *fait divers*, having taken over in newspapers and on the radio, naturally moved on to television, starting cautiously and quickly expanding. *Faits divers* dominated television news, distracting audiences from issues that might anger the powers that be. They proliferated on special broadcasts. But stark images of people at their most banal, ugly, and stupid, depicted in distasteful settings, tended to get in the way of the stories.

Most of the time, it doesn't take much for a reporter to organize reality, to make things cohere and respond to whatever questions might arise. After the assassination of President Kennedy, televised live, and the murder of Oswald by Ruby, also shown live, the crimes were broadcast and rebroadcast dozens of times to viewers who probably had no need to see them so often. Those images didn't add an ounce of clarity to a chain of events that was never elucidated. Getting close to the material truth of an event does not bring television any closer to its meaning.

Another boundary crossed: when the reporter Raymond Depardon films a real police station, he acts just like a feature filmmaker. He composes a narrative by playing with the passage of time. For example, a woman who has just pressed charges in the most ordinary fashion is revealed little by little to be completely deranged.

Journalists are of one mind with the courts and with most of the public. They all want human beings to be logical and to commit only logical actions, even if those actions are criminal. They weigh the act committed in a moment of passion on the scales of reason. They'll do anything to make the sad hero of the crime tale act in character so they can then come up with a rational explanation for his case. They are like Marcel Proust, who tried to understand the "Filial Sentiments of a Parricide" and asked in vain how Henri Van Blarenberghe, a loving son, could have succumbed to a murderous frenzy and killed his mother. I tend to think more like Paul Valéry, who said that crime is located first and foremost in the unconscious.

Fait divers, literally "a diverse happening": according to the *Trésor de la langue française*, the term has existed since 1859. Ponson du Terrail uses it in volume 5 of his *Rocambole*. In his *Walks in Rome*, in 1829, Stendhal introduces the English word "reporter." As for the reports themselves, you find them as early as 1865. In Italian, *faits divers* are called *cronaca nera*. A chronicle that delivers the ration of atrocities we hunger for every day of the week. Baudelaire and Proust have spoken of this daily pleasure.

Baudelaire: "It is impossible to scan any periodical, from any day, month or year, without finding evidence on every line of the most appalling human perversity, together with the most surprising boasts of probity, goodness and charity and the most shameless assertions concerning progress and civilization. Every newspaper, from first line to last, is a tissue of horrors . . . and this is the disgusting beverage that civilized man drinks with his breakfast every morning. Everything in this world sweats crime: the newspaper, the walls, and men's faces. I do not understand how any clean hand can touch a newspaper without wincing in disgust."

And Proust (quoting Baudelaire along the way): "Moving on to that abominable and voluptuous act known as *reading the paper*. . . . No sooner have we broken the fragile band that wraps *Le Figaro*, and that alone separates us from all the miseries of the world, and hastily glanced at the first sensational paragraphs of which the wretchedness of so many human beings 'forms an element' (those sensational paragraphs, containing what we shall later recount to those who have not yet read their papers), than we feel a delightful sense of being once again in contact with that life with which, when we awoke, it seemed so useless to renew acquaintance."

The *fait divers* is murder considered as one of the fine arts. Everyone who reads a newspaper resembles those members of the Society of Connoisseurs in Murder that De Quincey talks about. When they read about an atrocity, they judge it "as they would a picture, statue, or other work of art." A perverse pleasure, although those who enjoy a beautiful *fait divers* carefully stop short of justifying murder, discouraged by the law of the land. They are not accessories to the crime, merely voyeurs. (De Quincey was editor-in-chief of the *Westmorland Gazette* in 1818 and 1819. He filled the paper with murder stories and accounts of criminal trials.)

The *fait divers* requires two artists: the criminal and his victim, since, as De Quincey remarks, "two blockheads to kill and be killed" have never produced anything of real interest. He adds disdainfully, "as to old women, and the mob of newspaper readers, they are pleased with anything, provided it is bloody enough. But the mind of sensibility requires something more.

There's the assassin and his victim, but let's not forget the third party, the indispensable reporter, who, like a new Theramenes, transforms the event into a beautiful story."

You would think that death was the only topic that interested anyone.

As the ghostly, nameless reporter says in Faulkner's *Pylon*, by way of encouragement: "Let's move. We got to eat, and the rest of them have got to read. And if they ever abolish fornication and blood, where in hell will we all be?"

The reporter is fascinated by the lives and loves of a ragged trio of aviators. His editor-in-chief quips that the newpaper doesn't need a Sinclair Lewis, a Hemingway, or a Chekhov on staff because the readers expect information, not a novel. His editor-in-chief doesn't have it quite right, because this reporter has a "genius for catastrophe." Drama flourishes wherever he goes. In the beginning, when the editor is scolding him, the three aviators, two men and a woman, have nothing to offer from a journalistic point of view. But the moment the reporter pays attention to them, death comes along, as the plane makes its turn around the pylon. They become the heroes of a completely conventional *faits divers*, obeying all the rules of the genre.

Stereotype is the word. In an article from 1946, Claude Roy is already complaining about the dominance of radio and of newspapers like *Paris-Soir*. He accuses them not so much of propagating immorality as of leaving us no choice, imposing a uniform perversity on everyone: "What threatens readers of *Paris-Soir*, moviegoers, and the people who listen to the national radio stations isn't just the constant eroticism they're fed, but the fact that they are no longer allowed to choose their favorite weaknesses freely from the rich palette of mortal sins, nuanced according to character, temperament and taste."

Readers love clichés. So do the standard figures of the *fait divers*: public enemy, jealous wife, ingenious con artist, thief who thinks he's Arsène Lupin:[2] most of the time they conform to a well-established role and stick to it until the day their felony is adapted for the stage, becoming the subject of the majestic costume drama that is played out in criminal court. I have often seen defendants behaving like bad actors, rising up to bellow their ready-made lines: "Ladies and gentlemen of the court, ladies and gentlemen of the jury!" As for the judges, prosecutors, and lawyers, their dramatic gestures and vocal effects, which are their bread and butter, become second nature to them.

When I was working as a journalist, I occasionally wrote up a *fait divers* in the middle of the night, with nothing but the wire service dispatch as my source. A possessive woman murders her radiologist ex-husband in a restaurant. He had left her five years earlier, and she had continued to pursue him with her hatred or her love — whatever you want to call it. The situation was so common that very little information was required. It was easy for me to invent everything, if you can call it inventing, by borrowing from the most ordinary rules of psychology and transposing a discreet echo of my personal woes to make it more convincing for the reader. In the ensuing days, as the investigation shed new light on the case, what I had imagined the first night about the feelings and motive of the murderess turned out to be accurate. This woman had made her husband's life unbearable. She had always been mean. But people who are mean don't realize it. She couldn't admit it was her fault that her husband left her. She preferred to continue stalking him, harassing him. And when she blew his head off with a hunting rifle, she told herself that now he could never leave her. He was hers forever. My feat wasn't so

2. Arsène Lupin is the gentleman thief in Maurice Leblanc's early detective novels.

impressive. In love as in hate, this murderess hadn't shown much originality. Whenever you use myth as a starting point for invention, you find reality.

The star of the *fait divers* is often a mediocre fellow of below-average intelligence — otherwise he wouldn't have been caught, or would have found a solution other than killing or stealing to resolve his problems — and he's the first one surprised and delighted to find himself transformed into a hero. He's "gotten into the papers." A waitress in a restaurant in the provinces told me how she collapsed on the street. When she was revived, a bottle of sleeping pills was found in her purse. The reporters concluded that she had wanted to end her life and printed the story in the local paper. As though she were watching a film, she was stupefied to recognize herself in the role of the heroine. Turned into a statue.

In *The Man Without Qualities*, Musil says of the assassin Moosbrugger, "his flattered vanity regarded these moments as the high points of his life."

Once their acts, their personalities, are transformed by the media and dissected by the gigantic legal machinery, the defendants, who scarcely recognize themselves, feel as if some transcendent force has taken over their lives. Like Dmitri Karamazov who, at the end of his trial, exclaims: "I feel the right hand of God upon me."

Like the novel, the *fait divers* is designed to help readers understand themselves. Or at least show them what they shouldn't do and which solution is the wrong one. It shows them the destruction of people who believed their situation had no solution other than someone else's death or their own death, or both. And what abysmal traps life can set for you.

Otherwise, this humble narrative genre obeys the same laws

that make literature evolve with our vision of the world. It used to be that insignificant *faits divers* were referred to as "dogs hit by cars." Television journalists now call them "trash cans on fire." I sense in this transition from the dog to the trash can, from the living to the inanimate, a depersonalization typical of our times. Just as, after World War II, at the height of existentialism, the exemplary crime story seems to have been the one that inspired Camus's play *The Misunderstanding.* Two innkeepers, mother and daughter, take to killing their guests and robbing them. The son (and brother) comes back from a long stay abroad and they don't recognize him. They murder him. Then they discover the truth. They kill themselves. There's not an iota of psychology in the story. Only an absurd situation. (Camus claimed that he was indifferent to "psychology" in the theater, at least as a playwright. And he put the word in scare quotes.)

Comparing the psychological crime story and the situational crime story, it strikes me that the latter was imbued with the postwar spirit. Nathalie Sarraute honored me by disagreeing in the opening page of her book of essays *The Age of Suspicion.*[3]

The crude criminal news item, once exploited by the journalist, occasionally benefits from supplementary distillation. Rendered sublime, quintessential, it makes its literary début. Roland Barthes, in his *Critical Essays*, shows how the *fait divers* is connected to the short story. In both cases, everything is self-contained: "its circumstances, its causes, its past, its outcome. . . ." You could go even further and argue that the *fait divers* is closely tied to the

3. Nathalie Sarraute's *The Age of Suspicion: Essays on the Novel* (New York: George Braziller, 1963) begins by arguing with Grenier's claim that the novel of the day, much like the news stories, favored Kafka's "homo absurdus" over Dostoyevsky's psychological dramas.

origins of the short story as a literary genre. In 1554, Matteo Bandello, a Dominican priest from Lombardy, published his *Novelle* [Stories], taken for the most part from real events and inspired by crimes and violent deaths. He was soon imitated in France by Pierre Boaistuau, who published his collection of *Histoires tragiques* in 1559. They departed from the spirit of Boccaccio's *Decameron* and Marguerite de Valois's *Heptameron*, generally considered the first short stories. From then on the genre would separate into two branches: light and cheerful stories on the one hand, and sentimental, tragic *fait divers* on the other. One of the great successes of the early eighteenth century, a book by François de Rosset, has an eloquent title: *The Tragic Histories of our Time. Containing the Fatal and Lamentable Deaths of Several People.* These short stories in a new style would find abundant primary source material in the *occasionals*, then the *canards*—the first versions of sensationalist journalism whose success suggests that the public in those days, as in our own, could never get enough blood and violence. A little later, the success of *Le Mercure Galant* was based both on *faits divers* and on short stories sometimes inspired by the former.

In the seventeenth century, newspapers also invented a surprising way of exploiting *faits divers*. They would recount them in more or less burlesque verse. These rhymes were first written for some rich patron, male or female. Soon, they appeared in print, in weeklies, for public consumption. Scarron, Jean Loret, Charles Robinet, La Gravette de Mayolas, Subligny are the best-known authors. Here is an example:

The other day a peasant lass
Riding by upon an ass,
On her way home, you see
To her place near Montmorency,

Having bought her goods,
Was waylaid by five hoods,
Who first robbed her purse,
And then, to make things worse,
Since she was young and fetching,
Raped the miserable wenchling. . . .

In Japan, in the eighteenth century, several of Chikamatsu's plays were inspired by real *faits divers*. Most astonishing is that he would sometimes write them only a few weeks after the event. Figuring out what writers take from real-life dramas is a never-ending task. Take Emma Bovary's suicide, inspired by the story of Delphine Delamare, whose maiden name was Couturier, and who died and was buried in Ry, Normandy. What else is there to know? How many people know nothing about Dante except the episode where Francesca da Rimini is murdered with her lover by her jealous husband? (Note that Francesca and Paolo were inspired in their adultery by another book, the love story of Lancelot and Guinevere, King Arthur's wife. Thus one *fait divers* inspires another, as long as it has been consecrated by literature, or at least by the popular press.). It is no accident that the story of Francesca and Paolo has produced so much commentary, not only from the romantically inclined but from Dante scholars, who are, after all, also romantically inclined. A Dante bibliography for the period 1891 to 1900 includes over a hundred studies of Canto V of the *Inferno*.

This relationship of the *fait divers* and literature was understood or at least perceived by the press. Before World War II, *Paris-Soir* sought to enhance its prestige by hiring writers— members of the French Academy, if possible—as star reporters. Among them were the Tharaud brothers. But Jérôme and Jean were known for being slow. The paper had to send a real journalist with quicker reflexes to accompany them on assignment. André Salmon tells about the time they went to Le Mans to cover the trial of the Papin sisters and sent in their dispatch from the trial four days late.[4]

Stendhal is probably the all-time champion of the *fait divers*. He devoured them in *Le Publiciste*, *Le Journal de Paris*, *Le Journal du soir*. He even believed they had medicinal properties. In *Lamiel*, when the young woman falls ill, Dr. Sansfin gets her a subscription to the *Gazette des Tribunaux*. "In less than a fortnight her extreme pallor seemed to diminish. . . ." Lamiel, by the way, ends up in love with and in cahoots with a bandit named Valbaire, a character based on Pierre François Lacenaire.[5] Stendhal, after reading his favorite newspaper, notes in his diary, on 24 messidor year XII (July 13, 1804):

> Still another example of the Othello catastrophe in Italy, near Genoa. A jealous lover kills his fifteen-year-old mistress, a rare beauty; he flees, writes two letters (invaluable testimonials — get them from Plana [a friend from Turin]); returns around midnight to his mistress's corpse, lying in her father's oratory, and there he kills himself with a pistol, the same way he killed her.
>
> Seek the truth about this deed.

He adds this strange conclusion: "That's the sort of thing that makes me realize more and more that mellow Italy is the land where people feel the most deeply, the land of poets."

4. Christine and Léa Papin, housemaids, were tried in 1933 for murdering their employer's wife and daughter. Their crime inspired Jean Genet's *The Maids*.
5. Lacenaire (1803–1836), a poet-murderer made famous by Marcel Carné's classic film *Les enfants du paradis* (1945).

Antoine Berthet's crime inspired *The Red and the Black*. Old crime tales copied onto manuscripts furnished Stendhal with material for his *Three Italian Chronicles* and with the set-up for *The Charterhouse of Parma*. Horrible stories like the one about the convent of Baïano offer, according to Stendhal, "unimpeachable facts about the human heart."

Starting with his first book, *The Lives of Haydn, Mozart and Metastasio*, each of his works regales us with some tragic *fait divers*. For his debut he borrowed freely from the history of the tragic love affairs of Stradella, a seventeenth-century singer, as recounted in Choron and Fayolle's *Historical Dictionary of Musicians*. Stradella fled Venice with his mistress, a Roman lady named Hortensia, and their lives became an endless flight from the assassins dispatched by Hortensia's jealous lover—a flight marked by extraordinary adventures. Which was how the assassins, moved to tears by the beauty of the singer's voice in the Basilica of Saint John Lateran, at first spared them. But the passing months and years did not extinguish the Venetian lover's desire for vengeance, and one day Hortensia and Stradella were found stabbed to death, in Genoa. Stendhal liked this *fait divers* so much that he embellished it in his *Life of Rossini*.

There are more *faits divers* in *The History of Painting in Italy* and in *Rome, Naples, and Florence*. The *Walks in Rome* are overflowing with *faits divers*. The most surprising is the preposterous appearance, right in the middle of this guidebook, of a very long account of a criminal trial that had just begun in Tarbes, France. Adrien Lafargue, a young man from Bagnères-de-Bigorre, was on trial for the murder of his mistress. A fascinating trial in fact, where the murderer was more sympathetic than his victim, which meant he got away with a five-year prison sentence. Before he was led out of the courtroom, he turned towards the public and exclaimed, "Brave and esteemed citizens of this city, I am aware of the tender interest you have demonstrated towards me; you shall live in my heart!"

Stendhal, or rather the court reporter whom he copied, added, "His weeping altered his voice. He was met with new applause, and the crowd rushed to his side."

This Lafargue affair would be one of the secondary sources for *The Red and the Black*. Only this time France, not Italy, was "the land of poets."

It is tempting to adopt the expression. The fantasized act that someone else dared to commit is transformed by paper and printer's ink into a notorious, sublimated, and ritualized deed—if only through the rudimentary act of some unknown reporter assigned to cover the police stations. What a trampoline for the imagination! Therein lies the paradox. Committed by a person devoid of imagination, it stimulates ours. The *fait divers* in its entirety is indeed "the land of poets."

WAITING AND ETERNITY

I believe that I have experienced waiting in its purest form, by which I mean waiting without waiting for anything. Waiting for nothing. I'm certainly not alone. There are actually millions of us, since this kind of waiting is the essence of military life. You're a soldier. You hear them shout "Fall in!" You're lined up, marched to the other end of the barracks. And there you're told "Wait!" For what? You have no idea, but you really don't care since you're indifferent to everything. In the end there may be a chore, or perhaps none at all. The best moment in a soldier's life is when he is snoozing on his cot, waiting to be called, to line up and hear "Wait!" This is waiting for waiting.

The grunt in his uniform, appearances notwithstanding, resembles those characters in Piero della Francesca who demonstrate through their very indifference that they live in the eternal present of those with neither a past nor a future. They exist, that's all.

The limbo of military existence, which includes moments of waiting with no purpose, is itself nothing but a very long wait, one of those typical fragments of life that we consider unworthy of being lived and that we put in brackets, telling ourselves that this isn't real life, that we'll begin to live, or to live again, later, or some other time. I can't remember outside which barracks two of us grunts were assigned to till a flower bed. My partner was a Corsican shepherd, whom we all appreciated because he was so down-to-earth. He had the good sense to stay put, and rested his chin on the handle of his spade. A sergeant came by and asked, "What are you waiting for?"

The shepherd grew indignant to the marrow. He couldn't have been more eloquent. "What am I waiting for?" he cried out, "He's asking what I'm waiting for? I've been waiting for three years for my goddamn discharge!"

Waiting is what you erase from your existence. That's where you fool yourself, as a popular tale shows in a striking way. A child gets a bobbin of magic thread. Whenever he wants to advance the course of his life, all he has to do is pull a little on the thread. So as soon as he is sick of waiting, or whenever he is curious about what will happen to him next, he pulls on the thread. At this rate, he ages very quickly and soon finds himself with an empty bobbin, at death's door. That's what happens, it seems to me, when you refuse to acknowledge the days without event, the hours of waiting.

Impatience is waiting's most constant companion. Impatience shadows waiting more often than stage fright dogs an actor before a play or a student before an oral exam, more often than anxiety accompanies anyone, sick or accused, who waits for a medical or legal verdict.

Meursault, in Camus's novel, shows that he is truly "strange" because, before the verdict, waiting means little more to him than the passing of time. No emotion, no anger. "There we all were, waiting . . . We waited a long time—almost three-quarters of an hour, I think."

Whereas after Prince Myshkin is condemned to death, waiting is intolerable. His sentencing leads him to advance this paradox: "Just think: if there was torture for example, it would involve suffering and injuries, physical torment and all that would probably distract you from the mental suffering, so that the injuries would be all that you'd suffer, right up to the time you died. For after all, perhaps the worst, most violent pain lies not in injuries, but in the fact that you know for certain that within the space of an hour, then ten minutes, then half a minute, then now, right at this moment — your soul will fly out of your body, and you'll no longer be a human being, and that this is certain; the main thing is that it's *certain*. When you put your head right under the guillotine and hear it sliding over your head, it's that quarter of a second that's most terrible of all."

The prince concludes: "Perhaps somewhere in the world exists a man whose sentence has been read out, who has been allowed to suffer and then been told 'Off you go, you've been pardoned.' A man like that could tell us perhaps. Such suffering and terror are what Christ spoke of. No, a human being should not be treated like that."

It's obvious that you don't have to look very far to find this man who may exist, "somewhere in the world." He is none other than Dostoyevsky, sentenced to death on December 22, 1849, and subjected to a full execution ceremony. This is how he described it to his brother Michael: "They took us to Semyonovsky square. There, on the spot, they read us our death sentence, we were given the cross to kiss, they broke our swords over our heads and outfitted us for death (white shirts). Then three of us were put on the scaffold for the execution. They called us by groups of three. I was in the second group and so I had only a minute more to live."

In *The Idiot* he describes the last moments of a man condemned to death not once, but twice.

For symmetry's sake, I can report what an extraordinary fellow once told me in confidence. He had worked as assistant executioner for Deibler, Desfourneaux, and Obrecht — three generations of henchmen in charge of the guillotine in France. He loved the first henchman and the third one, but not the second, about whom he said: "He's nuts about the guillotine. He can stay home for days at a time, sitting on his chair, clad in his hat and raincoat, waiting for a directive from the Minister of Justice."

Another death sentence story appeals to my imagination since it took place the day I was born. On September 19, 1919, while D'Annunzio was clowning around in Fiume,[6] a spy named Pierre Lenoir was put to death. World War I was over, but traitors were still being executed. *Le Journal* reported sadistically: "Let us recall that Pierre Lenoir was sentenced to death last May 8. He has been waiting for 139 days. Pierre Lenoir has believed for some time now that his sentence would be commuted. After a period of intense worry, he suddenly decided his life would be spared and his sleepless nights and nightmares gave way to a peaceful rest. Last night he went to bed calm and fell asleep. Certainly he was still hoping."

Entire lives are spent under the illusion that nothing has begun. In the last scene of *Uncle Vanya*, Sonia cries out: "We shall rest! We shall hear the angels. We shall see heaven shining like a jewel. We shall see the disappearance of evil and all our pain in the great pity that shall enfold the world. Our life will be as peaceful and gentle and sweet as a caress. I have faith; I have faith. My poor, poor Uncle Vanya, you are crying! You have never known what it is to be happy, but wait, Uncle Vanya, wait! We shall rest. We shall rest. We shall rest."

6. In 1919, protesting the Paris Peace Conference, the decadent writer and sometime war hero Gabriele D'Annunzio led the seizure of the city of Fiume, in Croatia, and declared it an independent state with himself as "Duce."

All Chekhov had to do was put his characters' lines in the future tense to make them reek of despair. The creatures in his plays and short stories are the ultimate heroes of waiting. When they can't stand it any longer, they cry out, "To Moscow!" But few succeed in leaving.

This is because waiting is both hope (in Spanish *espera* is not very different from *esperanza*) and resignation. In one of the essays in *Nuptials*, "Summer in Algiers," Albert Camus writes: "From the mass of human evils swarming in Pandora's box, the Greeks brought out hope at the very last, as the most terrible of all. I don't know any symbol more moving. For hope, contrary to popular belief, is tantamount to resignation. And to live is not to be resigned."

Another champion of waiting is John Marcher, the main character in Henry James's *The Beast in the Jungle*. From his earliest youth, he has the feeling that he's destined for something rare and strange, for some terrible, prodigious possibility that will emerge sooner or later and that will probably overwhelm him. By virtue of waiting for the Beast, "He had failed, with the last exactitude, of all he was to fail of." Suddenly he understands the meaning of waiting. He had been the man to whom nothing must ever happen. He missed out on the woman he loved and who loved him in return. That was the Beast that struck him.[7]

For Henry James, waiting is a nearly constant and varied source of inspiration that adds up to a philosophy of the "too late."

In Baudelaire's "Dream of a Curious Character," the poet waits

---

7. You can find the same theme treated more crudely in Dino Buzzati's famous *The Tartar Steppe*. Apparently he was inspired by observing his colleagues at the *Corriere della Sera*, seasoned journalists who'd spent their lives looking for a scoop.

for death: "I seemed a child, so keen to see the Show / He feels a deadly hatred of the Curtain. . . ." But nothing happens: "The curtain rose—and I stayed waiting still."

Doesn't Kafka express the inevitable disappointment that comes from waiting when he writes to his family: "In the end, the most likely is that we're going where we'd rather not go, and we're doing what we'd rather not do, and we live and die in a different way than we'd ever want, without any hope of a reward."

"Are we going to the lighthouse?" a child asks at the beginning of Virginia Woolf's famous novel. We know they won't go for another ten years, that the very fleeting moments of consciousness experienced by each character will finally accumulate into a huge block of time, and that by the end, several major protagonists will have died. But Virginia Woolf's consummate art and her very personal use of time prevent this novel about a ten-year wait for a walk from being reduced to just that.

Samuel Beckett gave us the title that has become synonymous with the value we place these days on waiting. But for Beckett, time is immobile or, at best, it comes in the circular form of an eternal return—an eternal return reduced to a "structure by refrain," as Ludovic Janvier calls it. "Will it not soon be the end?" Beckett's creatures say, when they don't shout—which is even worse: "Another happy day!" They're locked in time, "Balue's cage."[8]

Maurice Blanchot likewise suggests in his book with a syncopated title, *L'attente l'oubli* [*Awaiting Oblivion*]—that waiting is a

---

8. Jean Balue (1421–1491), a cardinal and minister to Louis XI, was imprisoned for eleven years for plotting against the king, though not, as legend has it, in an iron cage.

value in and of itself: "However important the reason for waiting, it is always infinitely surpassed by the process of waiting."

André Gide's effervescent *Fruits of the Earth*, where waiting is merely annoying and meaningless, now seems dated: "How long, O waiting, will you last? And once over, what will be left to live for. 'Waiting! Longing! For what?' I cried. 'What can come that is not born of ourselves? And what can be born of us that we do not know already?'"

Conrad's short story "Tomorrow" is about perverted waiting. "It's all tomorrow, then," repeats Captain Hagberd, former sailor and widow whose son Harry has disappeared. The captain has settled in the little port town of Colebrook, convinced that his son will return. His neighbor is Carvil, a blind man who lives with his daughter Bessie. The invalid behaves like a tyrant, screaming at her constantly. The townspeople make fun of Hagberd, an eccentric, a real madman. Bessie is his only friend, and little by little she comes to share his delusions. She falls in love with the missing boy and imagines that when he returns, she'll marry him. It helps her tolerate her father's brutality: "You are not an impatient woman, my dear," Captain Hagberd tells her.

Then a young man appears and indeed he's none other than Harry, the son. But the old man refuses to see him and keeps saying he's waiting for his son "tomorrow." He wants to smash the intruder's skull with the garden spade. Bessie, in conversation with Harry, tells the young man her strange thought: "It is *you* who come tomorrow." Seeing that his father and the young woman are both deranged, he replies, "But why won't today do?"

He ends up figuring it out: "Awkward this, eh? . . . It's all tomorrow, then, without any sort of today, as far as I can see."

Harry is a rolling stone who has wandered the world without ever being able to settle down, who has never stayed with the same woman more than a week, who likes his chums, his liquor, his gambling. He explains that his father wanted him to be a lawyer's clerk and that's why he ran away. He hasn't come back to be shut in or be married, only to borrow five quid. As soon as Bessie gives him a little money—all the money she has—he leaves. That's when Captain Hagberg explodes with joy at having got rid of "that 'something wrong.'"

The young woman returns to her horrible blind father, her hell. "It was as if all the hopeful madness of the world had broken out to bring terror upon her heart, with the voice of that old man shouting of his trust in an everlasting tomorrow."

Not many writers know how to deal with waiting as successfully as Boccaccio, during the great plague that ravaged Europe in 1348. We know there were ten young people—three men and seven women—who fled Florence for the countryside, in Villa Palmieri, in Fiesole, where they entertained one another, passing the time by telling a hundred stories, *The Decameron*. As Antonin Artaud put it, Boccaccio, with his "two well-endowed companions and seven women as lustful as they were religious. . . ." waited patiently for the plague to take its leave.

Some people take pleasure in waiting for what will never happen, what can't happen. Alain-Fournier confessed his tormented love affairs to his sister Isabelle and his brother-in-law Jacques Rivière in a letter dated October 19, 1910: "There it is: this woman has returned. She waited for me on a bench on the street for one evening, two evenings, ten evenings. She said: 'Time passes quickly when you're sure the person you're waiting for isn't going to come.' Once she even fell asleep."

Alain-Fournier was an expert, since he had spent days and weeks and years waiting for Yvonne de Quiévrecourt, the woman who inspired his novel *The Lost Estate* [*Le Grand Meaulnes*].

"Formally speaking, masochism is a state of waiting; the

masochist experiences waiting in its pure form," writes Gilles Deleuze.

Mrs. Raddick's daughter, Katherine Mansfield's "Young Girl," behaves on the outside like a capricious spoiled girl, but ends up stammering:

> "I—I don't mind it a bit. I—I like waiting." And suddenly her cheeks crimsoned, her eyes grew dark—for a moment I thought she was going to cry. "L—let me, please," she stammered, in a warm, eager voice. "I like it. I love waiting! Really—really I do! I'm always waiting—in all kinds of places . . . ."

She makes this speech on the front steps of the casino where her mother has gone to gamble.

When waiting becomes a habit, it takes on an odor, a color, connected to the light of the sky, the neon of a café, the shadows of a room, the noise of footsteps on a sidewalk. . . . Waiting makes us into Pavlov's dogs, for whom a certain odor, a certain color, a certain noise resonates, plunging us into an anguish as new and as old as our unhappiness.

Some men and women thus cultivate impossible love affairs, eternally secret passions. Waiting in love brings them more delight than the accomplishment of love. A silly ditty from the 1930s has some truth to it:

> Je t'attendrai
> Tu m'attendras

Even truer is the Jacques Brel song where a man waits eternally for Madeleine, "Madeleine qui ne viendra pas."

Annie Ernaux's *Simple Passion* describes in clinical detail the type of relationship whose essence is anguished waiting: waiting for a phone call, for a visit that may or may not happen, who knows when. "From September last year, I did nothing else but wait for a man. . . ." Ernaux sums up her alienation: "I would have liked to have done nothing else but wait for him." It's rather common-place to see passion flourish between two people whom every-thing separates. Chained to lives they can't relinquish, sometimes living thousands of miles apart, they still want to believe in the beauty and in the truth of feelings that torture them. Sometimes at the heart of their waiting they give in to other adventures, to fake passions, to interim affairs. You can cheat on waiting the way you cheat on hunger.

Thus they live double or triple lives, no longer knowing where to turn in their ever-expanding culpability. Lovers like these don't believe that the future belongs to them. They wait humbly for the distant moment of their aleatory and always brief meet-ings, for time stolen from everyday life. Love thus begins to re-semble a religion, with its secret altars hidden deep within the heart. It can last until death, which becomes nothing but one more hurdle. That day too, we will be separated. Who will be able gently to tell my lover that I no longer exist? In Chekhov's "A Boring Story," when Katia, who would only visit him briefly, finally leaves, Nicolaï Stepanovitch is about to ask her "So you won't be at my funeral?"

I once had a colleague of advancing years—a discreet, reli-able, and very married family man. He died suddenly. He was no sooner buried than a woman called the office. "I'm sorry to bother you. Is Mr. G. there? Today is Wednesday and every Wednesday, he comes to my place for lunch."

This woman had spent her life with a secret, waiting for Wednesday. She cheated time, apparently, by writing poems. *Cheating time!* What an expression. And *killing time!* Now there was no more reason to wait, but how could she have known?

Mr. G.'s mistress could not even read the obituary in the newspaper: she was blind.

Are the devotees of this type of love affair truly unhappy? I'm not sure. Madame du Deffand writes: "The only happiness I know is to be loved by what one loves, and although an eternal absence can be a terrible source of suffering, one tolerates it patiently when one can count on never being indifferent to that love."

In Flaubert's *A Sentimental Education*, Frédéric Moreau is happy to spend his life waiting for Madame Arnoux. And she is happy waiting for him. Isolated in Brittany, she spends her time contemplating the ocean: "I go and sit up there on a bench that I call Frédéric's bench."

She resembles the hero of one of Henry James's most beautiful short stories. Resigned to his defeat, his financial ruin, and his unhappiness, making no effort to struggle, Herbert Dodd sits down at the end of a jetty, facing the sea, on "the bench of desolation." In his case you can say that he is no longer waiting for anything.

Madame Arnoux is satisfied with a love affair that is nothing but waiting and frustration: "Never mind, we shall really and truly have loved each other!" She takes off her hat and Frédéric experiences the sight of her grey hair "like a punch to the gut." And when he suspects her of "having come to give herself to him," he feels an "indefinable feeling of repugnance, a sort of terror of incest," and he turns his back on her so as "not to tarnish his ideal." Waiting has transformed the object of his desire into an untouchable idol.

When the clock strikes eleven, Madame Arnoux decides to leave in fifteen more minutes. Another version of waiting. During fifteen perfectly empty minutes, "Neither could find anything to say to the other."

A thesis topic: "Compare Madame Arnoux's waiting with

Madame Bovary's waiting." Between the two of them, all there is to say about waiting has been said. They are the Bouvard and Pécuchet of waiting.

Since time is the very substance of the novel, it would be impossible to account for every novel in which the by-product of time — waiting — plays a major role. What could be more novelistic than Gatsby at night, alone in front of his house in West Egg, looking across the bay for a green light, because that's where Daisy Buchanan lives? With his "appalling sentimentality," as the narrator puts it, Gatsby projects into the future his regret about what hasn't yet happened: "Gatsby believed in the green light, the orgiastic future that year by year recedes before us . . . So we beat on, boats against the current, borne back ceaselessly into the past."

Apollinaire evokes the return of Ulysses:

His wife had been faithful to him
In the plush corner her loom at hand

Are we so sure of being the object of hope? It's the aspiration of those without love.

Yet we can read the ancient, venerable, and ever-poignant *Odyssey* as a poem about waiting. From that bed of pain where "my tears have streaked, year in, year out," Penelope waits for her husband Odysseus, then for her son Telemachus. The suitors wait for Penelope to make up her mind. Elpenor waits for a proper burial. As for Odysseus, prisoner of Calypso, then Circe, even Nausicaa, isn't his entire voyage marked by waiting? Towards the end, in Song XXIII, even Aurora, "dawn with her rose-red fingers," waits. She waits to replace the night, waits for Odysseus and Penelope to have stopped weeping and to have found "their bed, the old familiar place they loved so well." Waiting and movement are the paradoxical twins of *The Odyssey*.

The only person who doesn't wait in *The Odyssey*—after having waited a very long time, it's true, in *The Iliad*—is Philoctetes, shamefully abandoned on the Island of Lemnos because he was bitten by a snake and his infected wound gave off such a disgusting odor. The Greeks go back to get him because they need his magic bow to conquer Troy. He is one of the first to make it home. All these books. . . . It seems that one of the first acts inseparable from waiting is reading. Your eyes follow the length of a line and your mind waits for your eyes to advance, impatient to know what will happen next. But you have to be patient.

I often have a dream that I can't quite figure out. I dream that I am reading. I decipher the page, or even the line, word by word. How can it be that I, the author of the dream, if you can say such a thing—how is it that I don't know what comes on the next line, on the part of the page that I haven't read yet?

Tyrants hate most to wait. Take Louis XIV, who said, "I was forced to wait." This was about his carriage. Waiting can be understood in terms of power. In any meeting there is the person who is waiting and the person who makes him wait, who has the satisfaction of being waited for.

For the line fisherman, waiting is a sport.

For the man hunting his prey, waiting means identifying with death. He's on the lookout for the moment when his victim arrives in his sight line.

For some people, waiting means waiting for the right time. Like the pope's mule.[9] To stay in the ecclesiastical world, consider Father Meslier, who lived in the age of Louis XIV and Louis XV, and who spent his entire humble existence preparing his time

9. "The Pope's Mule," a 1925 story by Alphonse Daudet, is about a mule who waited seven years to deliver a vengeful kick to a young man in the pope's court at Avignon who had tormented him.

bomb, a will and testament in which he proclaimed his atheism and wished for "all the great men on earth and all the nobles to be hanged and strangled with the priests' guts." But during the sixty-four years of his life, he uttered nary a critical word.

Mink Snopes, one of Faulkner's more primitive heroes, waits thirty-eight years in Parchman Penitentiary, perfectly patient, because he knows that at the end of those thirty-eight years he'll do what he has to — seek his vengeance. Waiting occupies all his time.

But one must finally come down from literary paradise and back to everyday life, where truth isn't any truer than in books, just more difficult to bear.

The human condition: on Monday, you wait for the weekend, and on Sunday you can't stand the waiting for Monday. You wait for vacation and for vacation to end. You wait for retirement, all the while dreading it. You dream wistfully of the death of your partner, with whom you have waited too long. You don't wait for death, despite the fact that this is the only thing it would be reasonable to wait for, indeed to wish for.

And what to say about separation, so productive of great literature? After the war, a statistic went around: eighty-four out of every hundred repatriated prisoners of war got divorced.

Religions make extensive use of waiting. For good reason. According to Jewish belief, Judgment Day is supposed to take place in the Vally of Josaphat, also known as the Valley of the Desert or the Valley of the Decree. So people in a hurry went there to be buried, in order to be the first among the dead resuscitated. During a trip to Jerusalem, I took a walk in this vast cemetery. I was attacked by Palestinian kids throwing rocks. L'*intifada*, the ancient lapidation. A few more rocks and I too could have been in the first row, ready for the day I'm not waiting for.

Once it becomes an instrument of religion, waiting itself can become a religion, since we have built temples for it: waiting rooms. Strange places of worship, not of an unknown god, but of the void. There are first-class and second-class versions. Airports use a euphemism for luxury waiting rooms. They call them "clubs" or "lounges." Does the quality of waiting really change from second class to first? In train stations, the filth of the second-class waiting room, full of riffraff, has a compelling novelistic power.

To say that men are always ready to love a woman who "possesses the advantages of beauty," Pascal writes strangely in his "Discourse on the Passion of Love," "There is a place for waiting in their hearts."

The bureaucrat, the dentist, the doctor, the analyst, the physical therapist—all have created an image of the waiting room. This is the place where, beset by boredom, anguish, and impatience, we read magazines we'd normally be embarrassed to be seen with. And if by accident we mention them, we compensate quickly by adding, "I read it at the dentist's office."

What happens in waiting rooms deserves a sociological study. That's precisely what I did a long time ago, without any qualification whatsoever. I was a ghostwriter for an eminent plastic surgeon who wanted to write his memoirs. He was very conscientious, so he had me observe numerous operations: removing bags under the eyes, fixing noses, reconstructing breasts. He got it into his head that I should spend entire mornings in his waiting room, listening to what the patients were saying and observing their behavior.

I've never seen an atmosphere like it except at the vet's, where people are busy reassuring their animals, who are trembling in fear since they know exactly where they are. The owners speak to their neighbors, asking the name and the age of their dog or cat, and what illness they have. At the plastic surgeon's, it doesn't take much to start a conversation. The returning patients, who've come to have their scars checked or their stitches removed, take the new ones under their wing, reassuring them through the wisdom of their experience. With no fear of generalizing, I can say that you could detect a slight collective tendency towards exhibitionism. The woman proud of her new breasts could not always resist showing them off.

One image stays with me. A woman who was never satisfied with her nose, who had it constantly remodeled. She brought color sketches and made pronouncements such as, "I want nostrils that are flared enough to look sensual, but not so flared as to be vulgar." As soon as she arrived, she leaned against the window, ducking under the curtain to take advantage of the sunlight. She took a pencil and a mirror out of her purse. She stuck the pencil in her nostrils, trying out different shapes. This woman didn't talk to the rest of us; she was caught up in an ideal of beauty she would never achieve.

At the end of waiting, the adverb *enfin* — "at last" — indicates relief, according to the French dictionary. Alone at last! Or as Paul-Jean Toulet has written:

My nurse said that at last
Is the husband of at least.

You don't need to reflect for long about waiting to think of the waiting of those who no longer wait. I remember one of the last letters I received from my mentor Pascal Pia. It contained these heart-wrenching words: "*Acta est fabula*, but the curtain is falling a little too slowly."

Misery is when there is no more waiting possible. Jean Paulhan, in a September 1923 letter to Francis Ponge, writes about "the admirable prosopopeia of a missionary, I think it was Father Bridaine, who claimed that the damned never stopped asking 'What time is it?' and that a horrific voice never stopped answering, 'Eternity!'"

LEAVE-TAKING

The Declaration of the Rights of Man[10] created a blueprint for freedom. It contains seventeen articles. And it's not mere whimsy that leads me to cite Baudelaire, who jokingly added articles eighteen and nineteen: the right to contradict oneself and the right to leave.

Contradicting oneself and leave-taking: these two concepts invite us to reflect. They bring to the notion of freedom two essential elements: the right to contradict oneself and the right to leave. I am convinced that no better way will ever exist for an individual to practice a subtle yet irrepressible form of rebellion, completely self-contained.

Let's quote Baudelaire more precisely. He started with the right to contradict oneself. He wrote in Philoxène Boyer's scrapbook: "Among the rights discussed recently, we've forgotten one in which *everyone* is interested: the right to contradict oneself." He deposited this thought in Philoxène Boyer's scrapbook because this strangely named poet (who took his name from the

10. A founding document of the French Revolution, adopted in 1789 by the first National Constituent Assembly.

author of dithyrambes who lived in Cythera in the fifth century B.C.) was a real loudmouth. Baudelaire had Philoxène in mind when he wrote in "Solitude" about "individuals who would accept the supreme agony with less reluctance, if they were permitted to deliver a copious harangue from the height of the scaffold, without fear that the drums of Santerre would unseasonably cut short their oration." (Philoxène Boyer's scrapbook was auctioned off at the Nouveau Drouot in Paris on May 22, 1985. The bidding reached 500,000 francs.)[11]

In 1852, Philoxène produced a satiric review called *Feuilleton d'Aristophanes* [Aristophanes's show] at the Odéon Theater, starring Marie Daubrun. The actress was probably his mistress before becoming Baudelaire's mistress, then Bainville's mistress. But I digress.

In his preface to Edgar Allan Poe's *Extraordinary Stories*, Baudelaire adds the right to leave to the right to contradict onself: "In the long list of the *rights of man* which the wisdom of the nineteenth century keeps increasing so often and so complacently, two rather important ones have been forgotten, the right to contradict oneself and the right to take one's leave."

To take leave. The image is very satisfying. A person who is silent, timid, introverted, who never protests, never complains, opens the door one day and takes off. The very idea fills you with good cheer. But you need to read to the end of Baudelaire's page to understand: that is not the idea here. The sentence came to him in connection with the deaths of Edgar Allan Poe and Gérard de Nerval, which convey a very strong meaning for "leave-taking." It's not about going off one evening to buy matches and never

---

11. Accounting for inflation, that would be the equivalent of 128,800 euros, or $166,550, an astonishing sum for a document that belonged to a virtually unknown figure.

returning, but about suicide. In fact, although Edgar Allan Poe didn't actually kill himself, his death is "almost a suicide" for Baudelaire—a suicide long in the making. As for Nerval, he "left discreetly, without troubling anyone—so discreetly that his discretion resembled disdain—freed his soul on the darkest street he could find. . . ."

Baudelaire adds this comment: "But society regards the person who leaves as an insolent fellow, and would willingly punish certain mortal remains, like that unfortunate soldier, suffering from vampirism, who was driven mad by the sight of a corpse. And yet . . . sometimes, under the pressure of certain circumstances, and after an in-depth analysis of irreconcilable differences with the given dogmas and metempsychoses, it may be said without pomposity, and without playing on words, that suicide is at times the most sensible action in life."

What more delightful man was there in all of the nineteenth century than Gérard de Nerval? One of his contemporaries, Eugène de Mirecourt, portrays him as ". . . a frank and loyal face on which—a rare thing in this lowdown world—are reflected goodness, wit, finesse and candor all at once."

Where did it get him? Hanging by an apron string one bitter cold night and ending up in the morgue, "lying nude on a slab of zinc," where Maxime Du Camp saw him.

When the commentary and the sarcasm produced by these two deaths began to revolt him, Baudelaire claimed the right to take leave.

In the next century, Cesare Pavese would express the same sentiment.

> To wander through the lonely streets
> Continuously tormented by the terror
> Of seeing the long-desired creations

Vanish before my very eyes,
To feel passion, hope . . . everything . . . everything
Grow weaker within my soul.

Pavese was still a student at the lycée when he wrote this verse. The idea of leave-taking kept haunting him until the night in 1950, on a piazza in front of the Turin station, when he took a room in the Hotel Roma, with its large blood-red sign.

From the depths of his obsession, Pavese realized how difficult the act is, and he was surprised that the most humble beings could manage to do it so naturally: "And yet, pathetic little women have done it."

That night of August 26, 1950, he telephoned a few of his women friends who might have kept him alive. In vain. He died because none of them wanted to waste an evening with him.

It's come to light recently that the American actress Constance Dowling, Pavese's last unhappy lover, also ended her life in 1969, in Los Angeles, at the age of forty-nine.

If "leave-taking" is a right, it needs justification. The young Camus, in an astonishing statement, considered it the only truly serious philosophical problem. Novalis had already written "The true philosophical Act is the annihilation of self [*Selbstötung*]; this is the real beginning of all Philosophy."

Philosophical suicide is nonetheless rare. Its theory, among the stoics, breaks down into an obscure quarrel over good, bad, and "intermediate" values. I doubt anyone has ever wanted to kill himself for having heeded the Academy rather than the Portico. Jean Starobinski recalled that "in reality, suicidal acts are rarely attributed to a single and simple cause. They are over-determined." Often, a moment's impulse sets off a suicide. The day my friend Romain Gary killed himself, he called Geneva, where they were expecting him, to arrange a ride from the airport; he asked a nurse what medicine he should take; he had lunch with Claude Gallimard, his editor, to discuss taxes. He killed himself at the end of this ordinary afternoon.

Suicide is a precipice you walk along, which makes you more or less dizzy, depending on the day and on your mood. "It seems that one kills oneself as if in a dream," wrote the surrealists as they launched their famous survey on suicide. For some, afflicted with the "absurd vice" described by Pavese, playing with the idea of "leave-taking" becomes a way of life. "The idea of suicide is a protest against life; by dying, you would escape this longing for death." "What a death, no longer wanting to die," Pavese notes. And René Crevel: "Isn't being haunted by suicide the best deterrent against suicide?"

But he ended up killing himself.

Mallarmé is supposed to have said: "There's not a single day, as I walk up the rue de Rome, that I'm not sharply tempted to throw myself over the railroad bridge and have done with life."

The right to contradict oneself gets mixed up with the right to take leave when one wants to find reasons to stay or to postpone. You can believe that life isn't worth the trouble of living, but decide that obligations towards others keep you in this valley of tears. This is known as "having dependents." You can also kill yourself, not because life seems horrible, but because you love life so much that the idea of being deprived of it is intolerable. Short-sighted suicide. Even without getting to that point, many people curse life because it is spoiled by the perspective of death. Hugo von Hofmannsthal says about one of his characters: "He hated his premature death so much that he hated his life for having brought him to it."

And Michel Leiris, in *Aurora*: "Fearing death, I loathed life."

On the same theme, Jules Laforgue, in an article on Paul Bourget, recalls a little dialogue he claims to have had with him:

"Good day Mr. Bourget. Always sad. So, what is bothering
    you?"

"I have life."

"And what do you find so sad about life?"

"Death."

"Yes, indeed, try to get out of that."

Thus Paul Bourget, looking for a solution, condemned the same individualism he had lauded so forcefully in his Stendhal phase, which obviously brought with it too much torment, and he was reduced to seeking refuge in conventional belief systems: native soil, the army, religion, the monarchy. . . . When it comes to living, you justify it any way you can.

At the end of his life, Malraux remembered a character in *La voie royale* [The Way of the Kings] who refused to acknowledge any of life's moral or philosophical value: "There is no such thing as death; there is only I, who am about to die."

People have their good and their bad reasons for dying. It is true that the reason matters less than the act. The reason can be excellent or stupid; if the act succeeds, you're nothing but a cadaver, meaning you're nothing.

At the slightest argument, a certain member of my family used to get up from the table with great drama (usually the fights broke out during dinner) and wander through the streets, giving us the impression that the goal of running away was to end up at the bottom of the river. This person abused the right to take leave twice over. She made it into a form of reprisal and terror. She hoped that the fear of losing her would make us quickly run after her. In these moments, she also must have loved the image of herself that she was creating. The hereditary tendency to commit suicide, its frequency according to sex, age group, profession, social class, country, leads us to believe that although we have the impression we are choosing suicide, suicide is choosing us. In Mont-Gabriel, in the Laurentides, I was talking with the Belgian critic René Micha about Philippe Jullian, who had killed himself a few days earlier. It was a peasant's suicide by hanging, despite the fact that Jullian was the very arbiter of Parisian homosexual elegance. Suddenly René Micha, a rather slick character from whom I wasn't expecting to hear anything surprising, declared:

"My family is full of people who committed suicide. My father, my uncles. So I'm very aware of suicides, I recognize people who are going to kill themselves in advance. I put their names on a list. The day they do the deed, I cross off their name."

"Philippe Jullian, was he on your list?"

"Yes."

I think about Hemingway. His suicide can be classified as euthanasia. Ailing and afraid of losing his faculties, he preferred to end his life. But we might remember that his father had killed himself and that he used the same gun Dr. Hemingway had used. So not only did he want to spare himself the suffering and the humiliation of a life in decline. He may also have been trying to do what his father had done before him. It's easy to show that his entire work is imbued with what Pilar calls in *For Whom the Bell Tolls* "the odor of death-to-come."

Montherlant, in much the same way, threatened with blindness and afraid to end up at the mercy of doctors, chose to leave life while there was still time. But would he have chosen this solution if he hadn't always found strength in reading the Romans and if they hadn't given him an exalted idea of voluntary death?

After Montherlant's suicide, something strange happened. The newspapers, in a perfect demonstration of the right to contradict oneself, changed their tune about him by suddenly admiring him for making his behavior conform to his writing. Even the Catholic press, the most high-minded of all, not only praised him for taking this action, but went on at length in praise of suicide.

All it takes is for someone you know to commit suicide to make the treastises sound indecent. They're nothing but words strung together, whereas the person you know paid with their life. Instead of funeral orations, someone might have found a way to save them, not just from death, but from solitude and distress. I understand Francis Jamme's reponse to the survey on suicide in *The Surrealist Revolution*: "The question you pose is absolutely pitiful, and if ever a poor child kills himself because of it, it is you who will be the murderer."

The same survey moved Pascal Pia to formulate a similar response, but for different reasons: "A poor man, I have no desire to love the poor. Those who were moved to commit suicide by their convictions or lack of convictions were born to be victims one way or another. I take no stock in giving the charity of my love to indigent ghosts. Suicides always seem to me in some sense the expiatory victims charged with paying the ransom, the debt, for a world they had no part in making. It's a disgusting role, I don't want to play it."

Even if you don't want to dwell on the issue and prefer the more ordinary meaning of leave-taking, there is something basic going on here. The right to put an end to your life is an individual liberty. As with all liberties, it amounts to a fight against the Church, the State, against anyone who pretends to have exclusive rights over our lives. It is an individual response to society, and perhaps we ought to study why this right has taken on a particular meaning for a good many writers. What significance should we give the frequent suicides of twentieth-century Japanese writers Akutagawa, Osamu Dazai, Mishima, Kawabata, among others?

I can't remember in which society suicides and those who

committed suicide were punished by being exhibited nude on racks. The hope was that prudery would restrain people's desire to kill themselves.

There's not always a very big difference between the two meanings of "leave-taking." Tolstoy, as a very old man, traveled far from home to meet his death.

You can't speak in a light-hearted way about the right to leave. Whereas the right to contradict oneself is basically more whimsical.

When Stendhal says that spinach and Saint-Simon were his most abiding tastes, he is expressing the perpetual mobility, the inevitable changes of heart of a lively soul who, from one moment to the next, excoriates what he has adored, adores what he has excoriated, and congratulates himself. Who delights in a single instance of his faithfulness (towards spinach and Saint-Simon) and in his inconstancy (towards all the rest)

Montaigne said, intending no insolence, "I give my soul now one face, now another, depending on which direction I turn it."

In Louis Guilloux's novel *Le Sang noir* [Black Blood], the hero, or rather the antihero, says that the only liberty man has is to contradict himself.

Contradicting ourselves is something we take for granted, an experience we repeat daily. Many people will remember the famous sketch by the comedian Raymond Devos, where he laughs and cries about the same event as it strikes him one way or another. As for me, sometimes I even laugh and cry for reasons that are completely at odds with one another.

Since Freud, psychology has taught us how little we control our ego and to what extent its very unity is illusory. Instead, we are a battleground where opposing forces face off. The right to contradict oneself amounts to helping people accept who they are—beings struggling with several different impulses, some conscious, others hidden. Since everyone is the plaything of these various determinisms, each person must be taught to use their various aspects to find some semblance of freedom within themselves.

Certainly few men have the courage to question the unity of the self. I knew one, Emmanuel Berl. Though he was close to Bergson, who always spoke about duration, Berl felt disjointed, fragmented. He compared himself to a *millefeuille*—a many-layered pastry. All those fragments of self, pushing him into contradictory activities through which he couldn't perceive a single individual. There was the writer, the political observer, the man who courted women, the man who cultivated anemones, who smoked cigarettes. Where in all this was the forenamed Emmanuel Berl?

The right to contradict oneself amounts to a shock for any philosophy, since what the philosopher seeks is unity. The headache starts with Heraclitus and his comment that you don't bathe twice in the same river. But Heraclitus makes an effort to set limits on eternal change. He invokes the notion of equilibrium, symbolized by the goddess Nemesis. With the dialectic, philosophy discovered a rhyme that both expresses and resolves universal contradiction.

In art, the need for contradiction produced the baroque. Eugenio d'Ors discovered "the algorithm of the baroque" in the gesture of Christ rendered by Correggio in his painting *Noli me tangere*: "Oh Lord, Mary Magdalene at your feet implores you. You attract and refuse her at the same time. You hold out your hand saying: don't touch me. You show her the path to heaven by leaving her on earth, in her tender defeat. She too, a woman already repenting for her sins, still lascivious in repentence, is also, by definition, baroque. She who sits back on her heels to follow you, Lord."

We live our lives through the irreversible flow of time. No matter how much we despair, avoiding this fact is as impossible as it would be to return to our mother's womb. But time consoles us about time by offering us the right to contradict ourselves. It allows us to alter the principle of identity. We can't be both white and black. But we can be white, then black. Time is surprise, renunciation. The temporality of the I is the foundation of the mind's liberty.

With time we learn; we shed our prejudices and we progress. The men and women of my era have come a long way: from putting on gloves to go to mass, to congratulating themselves for fighting it out with the Huns, to always being afraid of getting a woman pregnant or catching syphilis (on this last point, fear has returned, with another name). . . . We used to live and think just as people did during the reign of Louis-Philippe. We had to contradict ourselves quite a lot to change our way of thinking.

Human life, which lasts longer and longer, outlives love. A life lasts longer than friendship, longer than literary, musical, or artistic taste. I have felt great passion for authors who no longer interest me in the slightest. Or else my interests have changed and are no longer expressed by those writers. Or I've spent so much time with them that it's no fun anymore. Or way too many people began to love them and it ruined the special affection I felt (which is not a noble feeling). Or else my frivolity deprived me of the courage to return to them and I could only venerate them from afar. Not to mention the gods of our childhood. Maturity makes us realize we have worshipped false idols. It was my misfortune to reread Alphonse Daudet — how I once loved him! The memory of my attachment is so strong that all I have to do is pick

up one of those old bound volumes we had at home. I had forgotten what was in them. My first impression was stronger than
reading them today. Who cares how condescending the author is
when he scolds and reproaches us, making us weep over his regiment of martyred children, unhappy cripples, and noble abused
women who parade behind their mascot, Little What's-His-
Name.[12] His so-called naturalism reproduces tried-and-true clichés rather than life itself—but what does it matter? What does
the real Daudet matter, since the Daudet of my childhood is more
real? The deadly Collège de Sarlande where Daniel is trapped as
a dorm monitor; Jean Gaussin carrying Sapho in his arms; Father
Gaucher casting his spell; and Monsieur Joyeuse, that gentle
dreamer: I loved them and it was painful to give them up in the
name of good literary taste.

That's not even counting all I didn't know and have learned
since about the kindly author of *Lettres de mon Moulin*. Alphonse
Daudet was a ferocious anti-Semite, the helpmate and supporter
of Édouard Drumont. Alphonse, a fitting father for Léon.[13]

Ideas also get tired—or tire us out. I used to have all sorts of
theories about voluntary servitude, La Boétie, T. E. Lawrence,
etc. Now I don't give them a second thought. For ages I longed to
possess the unabridged English edition of *The Seven Pillars*, illus-
trated by the author. But I was broke. Later I found it in a used
bookshop and I had enough money on me to buy it. But I was no
longer interested.

---

12. Le Petit Chose, or Little What's-His-Name—the nickname of the main
character and the title of Daudet's 1868 novel, based on his own difficult experience as a boarding school monitor.
13. Édouard Drumont (1844–1917), virulent anti-Semitic crusader, author of *La
France Juive* [Jewish France]; Léon Daudet (1867–1942), polemicist and editor of *L'Action Française*, Charles Maurras's nationalist-monarchist newspaper.

The most radical and cruelest contradiction is oblivion.

Time imposes narrower and narrower choices on us, ultimately irreversible. The anguish of adolescence is in having to choose, i.e., having to give things up. You can't be at the same time a fireman, an aviator, a professor, a vet. . . . Later, if we stop what we're doing even for a minute, we're likely to be reduced to tears at the thought of what fate might have reserved for us, all the possible paths we had to abandon, all the possible lives. In the need to contradict oneself, you can see a consequence of what Georges Bataille called "the desire to be everything."

The contradiction or, if you like, the opposing tendencies that everyone harbors, are the ferment of much literary expression. The subject of *Hamlet* is the hero's swerving between action and interrogation. T. E. Lawrence seems to take Hamlet as his model. Sometimes he privileges the Arab rebellion, sometimes his interior torment. Dostoyevsky's characters wage an endless war against themselves. Each of these heroes invites us, simple readers, to wage our own interior combat.

Another notorious example: Flaubert. *A Sentimental Education* is a novel that undoes itself, since we learn in the end that the entire history of Frédéric Moreau, his dreams, his loves, his disappointments, mean nothing compared to the memory of an adolescent visit to a brothel. "Ah, that was our best time." A single sentence denounces and abolishes the beautiful novel we were taking at face value.

Flaubert ushers his contradictions down the path of derision. He agreed to write *Madame Bovary*, to suffer through the ordeal of rewriting the speech at the agricultural fair seven times, because his friends told him that *The Temptation of Saint Anthony* was a failure. Next, when he started *Salammbô*, you might imagine it was to avenge the mediocrity of the provincial world that had produced poor Emma. But he lets loose: "Few will suspect how depressed one had to be to undertake the resuscitation of Carthage!"

The most dejected confession that a literary creation ever inspired. What does the splendor of the Orient, History, dead civilizations amount to when compared to the melancholy of the reclusive man from Croisset?

Bouvard and Pécuchet uses derision in reverse. The father of the two idiots ends up being moved by them. However stupid they may be, the world is even stupider and soon they emerge as heroes of our times.

After so many doubts, negations, brusque changes of direction, we can understand Flaubert when he writes: "Ah! The anguish of style — how well I've known it!"

A whole family of writers has laid claim to derision — whether they know it or not. Joseph Conrad uses it on purpose. I'll only mention one short story, "A Smile of Fortune." It starts with a love story, with a creature as sublime as she is mysterious, on an island in the Indian Ocean that is compared to a pearl, and it ends with the account of the black market in potatoes.

Some writers have only given in to the demon in a single work, almost accidentally. Take *Pylon*, which differs from every other Faulkner novel. In this story of grace refused, of impossible love, of misunderstanding, the Faulknerian curse approaches the absurd. The ridiculous and pathetic reporter guarantees the misery of the aviators who fascinate him and the woman he loves, just by wanting to help them.

With Samuel Beckett, contradiction is condensed in a simultaneity that leads to a stuttering of thought. In *Molloy* he is miles from the clarity of Camus's "Today, Maman died" in the opening of *The Stranger*, though he's evoking an analogous situation: "For example my mother's death. Was she already dead when I came? Or did she only die later? I mean enough to bury. Perhaps they haven't buried her yet."

Anguish is nestled between sentences that hang like a swinging door.

For these authors, derision oscillates between living and judging life, between suffering and watching suffering. The only way the two attitudes can exist together is through self-condemnation. Then, from the depths of derision, a movement of self-pity brings a bit of sad tenderness. The writer has only to take up his pen. He seems put out, as though he were Uncle Vanya at the end of the play, defeated and starting to write in his book of receipts: "On the 2nd of February, twenty pounds of butter; on the 16th, twenty pounds of butter once more. . . ." Carried along by the interior flow that stirs up both his sorrow and the sublimation of his sorrow, he's now partially consoled.

At the end of the contradiction there's the temptation of silence. Why do we write? For whom? Can you be a writer without feeling the need to communicate? And isn't communicating, or refusing to communicate, one of the thorniest problems an individual faces?

"The refusal to communicate is a more hostile means of communication, but the most powerful," writes Georges Bataille.

What can we say about those who write to proclaim their solitude or their despair? Maurice Blanchot remarks, "A writer who writes 'I am alone,' or, like Rimbaud, 'I am actually from beyond the grave' can seem a little ludicrous. It is comical to be aware of one's solitude while addressing a reader, making use of the very means that prevent mankind from being alone."

The despair that accommodates beauty of style is not exactly despair. There is something suspect, as Blanchot says, about the writer who "[Makes] himself admirable by the expression of his suffering."

Silence has more subversive power than any speech, any writing. For Marcel Arland, "the rarest form of audacity is not destruction, it's abstention; there's more violence in saying: no, silence is it." As for myself, like so many others who have written too much, despite being tempted by silence, I remain haunted by the figure of Pascal Pia. In his youth, he finished a collection of poems, *Le Bouquet d'orties* [the bouquet of nettles]. Just as it was about to be published by Gallimard—this was in 1924—he withdrew the manuscript. There was nothing he valued more than literature, except silence. His refusal was antisocial, but why? Eddy du Perron, who portrayed him very faithfully as Viala in his novel *Country of Origin* (he also portrays Malraux, whom he calls Heverle), has him say—and the remark is doubtless authentic: "Talent emasculates you before you realize it. If your books are so great that the enemy admires them or awards them prizes, then it's over: you've become part of the literary establishment and you contribute only to the higher glory of national art."

If you're the least bit individualistic, this sort of thing gives you pause: the respectability of belles lettres, the greater glory of official culture. . . . It's true that the idea of playing those games is not appealing.

An adept at silence, Pascal Pia certainly had precursors, remarkable men who chose to remain in the shadows. But how would we know? We do know about one of them. Paul Challemel-Lacour (1827–1896) was a disciple of Schopenhauer who refused to publish his *Studies in Pessimism*. But the fact remains that this intense pessimist was also at various times in his life a high-level administrator, an elected official, an ambassador, a cabinet member. Pia often quoted Baudelaire's line about the right to contradict oneself and the right to take leave. I got it from him. You find it in Camus's notebooks, also inspired by Pia. If he were still alive, I think that this devout atheist would add the right to blasphemy, since today, in the name of nonsense and of divinities bound to fade as surely as the previous ones, believers of every stripe — some who lead their empires into war, others who issue death sentences — transform men and women into living bombs. All it took was the publication of a cartoon of their prophet in a distant land for them to set the streets on fire.

This was not yet the case a few years ago and Pascal Pia, after having added to the two rights claimed by Baudelaire the right to silence, demanded, at the end of his life, the right to the void. He forbade anything to be written or said about him after his death and even forbade the announcement of his death. And yet some of us who were his friends, faithful and treasonous, can't ignore his memory.

It's tempting to add a fictional character to this living example: Bartleby the Scrivener. Once cherished by a happy few, the hero of Melville's short story is quoted and exploited today by just about everyone on the planet. I still don't have the heart to give him up. Bartleby is not a writer in the ordinary sense, but a scribe, a copier, who answers everything with "I would prefer not to." Bartleby, who worked in the dead-letter office.

Dead letters! What a metaphor for the rest of us! If ever we need a patron saint to encourage us on the road to silence, I would recommend Bartleby in a heartbeat.

Some may think I've gone on way too long about the twentieth right, the right to silence, and that it's high time I put it into practice.

PRIVATE LIFE

The expansion of the media has put the writer in the spotlight, even if, nowadays, people who write have lost much of their prestige and their importance in society. Some of them find themselves afflicted with a lack of privacy once reserved for movie stars. Sometimes they ask for it. Michel Contat writes about "this form of media totalitarianism that gives the right to know everything about someone based on the simple fact that he or she has created a public image." This phenomenon is not so new, if you think about Sartre and Beauvoir, not to mention Musset and George Sand, Dante and Beatrice, Petrarch and Laura, or even the self-dramatizing Byron or Chateaubriand. Nowadays we have scribblers who manage to pass themselves off as writers because they've already made a name for themselves as celebrities.

Gérard de Nerval was a victim of the public's need to know, due to conditions that would be unimaginable today. Jules Janin, in the *Journal des débats* of March 1, 1841; Alexandre Dumas, in *Le Mousquetaire* of December 10, 1853; Eugène de Mirecourt in a little monograph in his series *Les Contemporains* in 1854, wrote openly about their friend's mental illness. Poor Gérard wrote to his father on June 12, 1854, in response to Mirecourt's pamphlet on "necrological biography," and said he was being made into "the hero of a novel." He dedicated *Daughters of Fire* to Alexandre Dumas: "I dedicate this book to you, my dear master, as I dedicated *Lorely* to Jules Janin. You have the same claim on my gratitude. A few years ago, I was thought dead, and he wrote my biography. A few days ago, I was thought mad, and you devoted some of your most charming lines to an epitaph for my spirit. That's a good deal of glory to advance on my due inheritance."

Is knowing the private life of an author important for understanding his or her work?

The debate was renewed with great panache by Marcel Proust in *By Way of Sainte-Beuve*. Proust noticed that Sainte-Beuve, a subtle and cultured man, made nothing but bad judgment calls as to the worth of his contemporaries. Why? Jealousy doesn't explain it. He couldn't have been jealous of writers like Stendhal or Baudelaire, who were practically unknown. The fault was with his method. Sainte-Beuve wanted to adopt a scientific attitude. "For me," he wrote, "literature is indistinguishable from the rest of man. As long as you have not asked yourself a certain number of questions about an author and answered them satisfactorily, if only for your private benefit and sotto voce, you cannot be sure of possessing him entirely. And this is true, though these questions may seem to be altogether foreign to the nature of his writings. For example, what were his religious views? How did the sight of nature affect him? What was he like in his dealings with women, and in his feelings about money? Was he rich? Was he poor? What was his regimen? His daily habits? Finally, what was his persistent vice or weakness, for every man has one. Each of these questions is valuable in judging an author or his book."

Sainte-Beuve decides that he is engaging in literary botany.

Proust finds all this knowledge useless and likely to mislead the reader: "A book is the product of a different *self* than the self we manifest in our habits, in our social life, in our vices. If we would try to understand that particular self, it is by searching deep within us and trying to reconstruct it there, that we may arrive at it. Nothing can exempt us from this effort of the heart."

Proust also writes: "How does having been a friend of Stendhal's make you better suited to judge him? It would be more likely to get in the way." Sainte-Beuve, who knew Stendhal and Stendhal's friends, found his novels "frankly detestable."

What Proust holds against Sainte-Beuve is that he made no distinction between conversation and the occupation of writing, "in which, in solitude, quieting the speech which belongs as much to others as to ourselves, we come face to face once more with ourselves, and seek to hear and to render the true sound of our hearts."

Proust admires Balzac, all while thinking that from what he knew of Balzac's personal life, his letters to his family and to Madame Hanska, he was a vulgar human being. Stefan Zweig raises the same issue. He admires Balzac the writer and seeks reasons to admire the man. He is infuriated because he can't find any. He has discovered that genius is incomprehensible.

Gaëtan Picon thinks that if Proust attacks Sainte-Beuve so violently it's because he needs to believe that genius is based on a secret distinct from intelligence. That a man whose life is frivolous and empty, a failure, can nonetheless create a great work. The question is inevitable, beginning with the case of Proust himself. How did this intolerable social climber, whom Lucien Daudet called "an atrocious insect," become the author of *In Search of Lost Time*? Paul Valéry concludes his famous study of Leonardo da Vinci with a line that shows in a striking way how much distance he puts between an artist and his work: "As for the true Leonardo, he was what he was."

Flaubert would have sided with Proust against his friend Sainte-Beuve. He writes to Ernest Feydeau on August 21, 1859, with his customary truculence, "Life is impossible now! The minute you're an artist, the gentlemen grocers, the auditors of record, the customs agents, the cobblers and all the rest enjoy themselves at your expense! People inform them as to whether you're a brunette or a blond, facetious or melancholy, how many moons since your birth, whether you're given to drink or play the harmonica. I believe that on the contrary, the writer must leave behind nothing but his work. His life doesn't matter. Wipe it away!"

He doesn't stop there, but insists: "The artist must arrange things so as to make us believe in a posterity he hasn't experienced."

You'd have to put Chekhov in Proust's camp. From his *Notebook*: "How pleasant it is to respect people! When I see books, I am not concerned with how the authors loved or played cards; I only see their marvelous works."

The same is true for Henry James, who writes in his short story "The Real Right Thing": "[. . .] his friend would at moments have shown himself as holding that the 'literary' career might — save in the case of a Johnson or a Scott, with a Boswell and a Lockhart to help — best content itself to be represented. The artist was what he *did* — he was nothing else." In this fantasy tale, the ghost of a dead writer appears to prevent his biography from being written.

Proust seems rigid. He is right to say that there is a truth for the writer, especially if he's a genius, that remains a mystery and cannot be explained by social appearance or private life. But he also presents a counter-argument to his own theory when he writes in *Jean Santeuil*: "[. . .] our lives are not wholly separated from our works. All the scenes that I have narrated here, I have lived through."

Most of the time, the characters in *Jean Santeuil* and the *Search* are indiscreet, eager to know everything about the artists they encounter. Freud, whose theory is close to Proust's, doesn't hold back from delving into the private life of Leonardo da Vinci and a few others. J.-B. Pontalis suggests with a touch of malice that Proust and Freud take the opposite tack to Sainte-Beuve's because they don't want their own private lives examined: if Proust's perversion of torturing rats was discovered. . . . The private lives of others are another story!

Nietzsche also pondered the question, but from a different point of view. He thinks that knowing an author distorts our opinion of his work and his person. "We read the writings of our acquaintances (friends and foes) in a twofold sense, inasmuch as our knowledge continually whispers to us: 'this is by him, a sign of his inner nature, his experiences, his talent,' while another kind of knowledge simultaneously seeks to determine what his work is worth in and of itself, what evaluation it deserves apart from its author, what enrichment of knowledge it brings with it. As goes without saying, these two kinds of reading and evaluating confound one another."

But what to do in cases where the work can only be explained by the life? Why deprive ourselves of this source of knowledge?

In the case of Albert Camus, once you know about his impoverished childhood in an illiterate milieu (he described this in *The Wrong Side and the Right Side*, his first book, and in *The First Man*, his last), you understand his attitude of respect and rigor towards literature, and the tenor of his style. In the same way, his youth near the sea and the sun, and the illness that continually threatened him, explain to a large extent the spirit of his work, his thought.

Finally — and Proust is right about this — if the author is not a simple manufacturer, if he puts his interior self in his books, the reader will be attracted by this self. The reader will seek out this personal, private self beneath the sentences.

In 1922, the young Aragon wrote, "My instinct, whenever I read, is to look constantly for the author, and to find him, to imagine him *writing*, to listen to what he *says*, not what he tells; so in the end, the usual distinctions among the literary genres — poetry, novel, philosophy, maxims — all strike me as insignificant."

Freud showed that every child constructs a "family romance" that he will later repress. Whereas the writer continues to manufacture a novel which, if not a family romance, is at least a personal one. Marthe Robert has noted that all novelists relate to some extent their *sentimental education*, their *apprentice years*, and their *search for lost time*. The paradox is that they confess their secrets to a piece of paper. Yet they're careful to disguise them as fiction.

Revealing a lot about oneself is not the purview only of novelists. It is also what poets do, and not just the elegiac poets. For centuries, and in a variety of civilizations, well before there were novels, the great majority of poems came from the poet's effusion in speaking about his life, his loves, his torments, his anger, his religious feeling, his exile. Gérard de Nerval asks, "Which is more modest: to portray oneself in a novel disguised as Lélio or Octavio or Arthur, or to betray one's most intimate emotions in a volume of poetry?" That his life and his illness were made public by his friends gave him an argument: "Forgive us our flights of personality, we who are constantly in the limelight, and who, whether we live in glory or in failure, can no longer hope to obtain the benefits of obscurity."

You might think that contemporary poetry, tending towards abstraction and situated in a world where the air is rarified, has little to do with private life. This is not always true. Even an erudite poet like Jacques Roubaud, who delves into mathematics, writes about a deeply personal unhappiness in *Something Black*.

The same is true for the playwright, the filmmaker, even the nonfiction writer. You can sense this clearly in the philosophers Jean-Paul Sartre, Michel Foucault, Roland Barthes. Descartes was already inserting elements of autobiography in *Discourse on Method*. In this essential essay, he portrays himself in Holland, seated next to his stove throughout the winter, reflecting. Thus there is a back-and-forth movement, a dialectic, practically a contradiction. One retreats into oneself in order to communicate better with others.

Authors, whenever they delve into their own private lives, even if they embellish or transpose, find themselves confronted with the issue of personal discretion. They go well beyond simple indiscretion when they attempt to bring to light what is hidden in the deepest part of themselves.

With his taste for nonsense, Julio Cortázar describes an "enlarged self-portrait from which the artist has had the elegance to withdraw." This little joke reveals the aspirations of so many writers: to be at once invisible and present, to say everything about oneself without seeming to.

Offering your essence to nourish what you write is what Scott Fitzgerald called "the price to pay": "I have asked a lot of my emotions—one hundred and twenty stories. The price was high, right up with Kipling, because there was one little drop of something not blood not a tear, not my seed, but me more intimately than these in every story: it was the extra I had."

Scott Fitzgerald couldn't write without including his entire history. And even when he lost his creative vein, he dug to the depths of his anguish to write *The Crack-Up*.

John Dos Passos, another American who is now neglected after having been overrated, made a distinction between a literature of confession and a literature of spectacle. Of course he categorized his own books *Manhattan Transfer* and the *U.S.A.* trilogy as literature of spectacle. But I'm pretty sure you can find confession beneath the spectacle.

The young novelist's first book is often autobiographical. Yet this is the phase when one has lived the least. Other, perhaps better, writers save the most personal, the most intimate in their lives or in the history of their families for much later.

On the other hand, some seem to write primarily to cover up a secret. Paul-Jean Toulet never shows his wounds — neither in his novels, frankly mediocre and marred by the most odious clichés of his era: anti-Semitism, etc. — nor in his poetry, far more charming; nor even in the letters he addressed to himself. His friends knew he had a broken heart. Why broken? And by whom? One of the qualities of his poetry is precisely that you can perceive, beyond the light-hearted fantasy, a floating veil of sadness or perhaps despair. We'll never know the whole story. That is the claim in the last quatrain of his *Contrerimes* — a kind of challenge:

> If living is a duty, when I will have ruined it,
> May I use my shroud as a mystery
> You must know how to die, Faustine, how to grow silent,
> Die like Gilbert by swallowing the key.

(The allusion is to the strange death at age thirty of the poet Nicolas Gilbert, author of the *Le poète malheureux* [the unhappy poet] who apparently swallowed his key in a fit of delirium.)

In the life of a man or a woman there are always one or two things that he or she will never consent to speak about, not for anything. Secret gardens. But if that man or woman is a writer, we might find those things hidden deep within a novel.

We know that Dickens lived through some very unhappy times in his childhood. The casual egotism of his parents was to blame.

His father, a loudmouth who was often imprisoned for debt, is in part the model for Mr. Micawber. In chapter eleven of *David Copperfield*, we find, barely altered, what Dickens experienced at age twelve. For six or seven shillings a week, he packaged shoe polish in a putrid factory, working under unspeakably miserable, humiliating conditions.

While he didn't hesitate to use this experience for *David Copperfield*, in life he hid the memory as his most closely guarded secret. He refused to talk about it. He even took detours in London to avoid the place where he had been so unhappy. A fragment of his autobiography was found where he confirmed:

> No word of that part of my childhood which I have now gladly
> brought to a close, has passed my lips to any human being . . .
> I have never, until I now impart it to this paper, in any burst of
> confidence with anyone, my own wife not excepted, raised the
> curtain I then dropped, thank God.
>
> Until old Hungerford Market was pulled down, until old
> Hungerford Stairs were destroyed, and the very nature of the
> ground changed, I never had the courage to go back to the place
> where my servitude began. I never saw it. I could not endure to
> go near it. For many years, when I came near to Robert Warrens'
> in the Strand, I crossed over to the opposite side of the way, to
> avoid a certain smell of the cement they put upon the blacking-
> corks, which reminded me of what I was once. It was a very long
> time before I liked to go up Chandos Street. My old way home
> by the Borough made me cry, after my eldest child could speak.

Thus Charles Dickens and David Copperfield, C. D. and D. C., meet in the person of a humiliated child. Humiliation is a feeling that very few people can tolerate. But it has inspired many books.

Léon Aréga, a forgotten writer who endured endless ridicule, once said to me about one of my novels in which I put much of myself: "It's a treatise on humiliation." Which, coming from him, was a great compliment. It is easy to find the humiliated child in many of Chekhov's short stories. His remark has been quoted a hundred times: "In my childhood, there was no childhood."

Confessions are made on purpose in *David Copperfield*. But in most novels they aren't. They surface in the form of fantasies, obsessions. With Dostoyevsky it's impossible not to find an allusion to the rape of a little girl in *The Possessed*, *Crime and Punishment*, *The Eternal Husband*.

One rather strange point of view comes from Joseph Conrad. He thought you needed to be a genius to dare unveil your intimate self and thus move the public. If the effect was ruined you would sink into ridicule:

> If it be true that every novel contains an element of autobiography — and this can hardy be denied since the creator can only express himself in his creation — then there are some of us to whom an open display of sentiment is repugnant. I would not unduly praise the virtue of restraint. It is often merely temperamental. But it is not always a sign of coldness. It may be pride. There can be nothing more humiliating than to see the shaft of one's emotions miss the mark of either laughter or tears. Nothing more humiliating! And that for this reason should the mark be missed, should the open display of emotion fail to move, then it must perish unavoidably in disgust or contempt.

This is what the authors of a fashionable genre, baptized "autofiction" in 1970 by Serge Doubrovsky, seem not to fear, and their works collect like dregs on booksellers' shelves.

Sometimes the most impersonal work can signify something deeply intimate to the author. This is the case of the great allegorical novel by Melville, *Moby Dick*. He achieves a fusion of a great myth with his own torment. The dire questioning, the violence of Ahab, are his. *The Plague*, another book that generates a myth, is also a novel about separation, since Camus wrote part of it isolated by the war, cut off from Algeria, from his wife, from his close friends. Virginia Woolf's *Orlando* seems like a fantastical novel of imagination, when it is really the portrait of Vita Sackville-West, who was so dear to the author. In a fairy tale like *Alice in Wonderland*, Reverend Dodgson confides his passion for Alice Liddell.

The sole fact of starting to write is motivated by a cause that belongs to what is most intimate for the author. I quoted Flaubert, who talks about the sorrow that launched him into the enterprise of *Salammbô*.

The critics always remind us that Proust and John Cowper Powys wrote their great novels only after the death of their mothers. You could say they waited for their mothers' deaths to write.

We mustn't forget the role of the unconscious. Benjamin Crémieux noticed that "the writer who rereads one of his books discovers, after the fact, secret traits he never suspected having put there, traits he may not even have known he possessed—and whose existence is suddenly revealed to him. In all that we write in our own style, the truest aspect of ourselves is inscribed in filigrain."

How, without blushing, can we agree to deliver to the public so many confessions and intimate motivations, even those that are disguised or dissimulated? This is the mystery of the quasi-religious value we assign to literature.

Novel and Memory

"Each artist preserves [. . .] deep down a single wellspring that nourishes what he is and what he says throughout his life," wrote Albert Camus, as he was looking to recapture the inspiration for his very first book, *The Wrong Side and the Right Side.* Writing is about trying to say one or two things, usually the same ones, from one book to the next. This is what Marcel Proust called the monotony of the work of art. To illustrate them, that is, to disguise them, you call on images drawn most often from memory. They can come from a very distant past. As Flannery O'Connor said, "anyone who has survived childhood has enough material to write for the rest of her life."

Memory itself is already a novelist. We know now that it is not a recording device, but that it is constantly recomposing the past. It invents more than it reconstructs. It is dynamic, nourished by our imagination, our personality, our passions, our wounds. It works that way for every human being and even more so for writers. Memory's inventiveness is more useful to them than its faithfulness. Which is why literary models never quite resemble the characters in novels. They were only pretexts.

As they age, humans certainly have a tendancy to freeze certain memories in stories *ne varietur* that they know by heart and replay word by word. To that extent everyone is more or less a novelist.

Finally, if I were asked what literary creation amounts to, I would say that it's about choosing among past and present realities. Faced with a character or a story, you say to yourself, "that one is for me, that one isn't for me." By that I mean it does or doesn't correspond to my sensibility, my way of understanding life, and finally to an esthetic, to a certain music that emanates from that esthetic. Memory obviously goes along with choosing and doubtless has already made its own choice.

The mysterious relationship of writers to their memories is something they safeguard with great care, because they are always afraid of destroying this source, or seeing it dry up. For most of them, a curious phenomenon takes place. They are obsessed by events, people, and places from the past. Which they use to write their book. Afterwards, it will become more and more difficult, if not impossible, to distinguish between what they imagined and what they remembered. Flaubert remarks, in a letter to Hippolyte Taine in November 1866, "the mental image of things is as true as their objective reality, and what has been supplied by reality very soon ceases, for me, to be distinguishable from the embellishments and modifications I have given it." Moreover, all it takes is for the book to be written and the part of the past that has haunted us for so long is erased from our memory. We don't think about it again. This is known as catharsis. The mind is purged. Thus, paradoxically, the novel succeeds in saving a bit of the past but also in destroying it. It devours memory. As Virginia Woolf was writing *To the Lighthouse*, she used her father and her mother for the first time. She noted in her journal, "But I wrote the book very quickly; and when it was written, I ceased to be obsessed by my mother. I no longer hear her voice; I do not see her." What is a novel, finally? It's a sort of mirror that reflects both the innermost life of the author and some aspect of the exterior world. It's a way of undoing reality in order to recompose it in another way, to give a truer image, by which I mean an image that can be useful to readers and can teach them something about the world and about themselves. Life in its raw state is often too incoherent, too mysterious as well, for us to be able to learn anything from it. Life, decomposed and recomposed through the prism of the novel, allows us to reflect. And brings us the satisfactions of an esthetic and emotional order, an outpouring of feelings.

I, Us, Him, Her

In the eyes of many readers, the use of "I" in a novel is synonymous with secrets, with confessions. Yet the "I" is usually no more than a literary device. It can be used in many different ways. "I" is sometimes a simple narrator, sometimes a witness, sometimes the main character. In Proust's *In Search of Lost Time*, the narrator is called Marcel, but this Marcel, whose name appears only three times—and even then only as a hypothetical name borrowed by the author for the sake of convenience—is not Marcel Proust. He's an actual character. Certainly they resemble each other. They even have in common a literary vocation. This "I" is in fact the cornerstone of the novel. It's what gives it perspective. The presence of a narrator makes it possible to look within a character while observing the entire scene. And if you look for Proust, you find him in the character of Swann just as much if not more as in Marcel.

In *The Stranger*, you'd expect the story of Meursault, a character who is absent to the world, to be told in the third person. But Camus chose to have Meursault say "I," to place us at the heart of that character's interior desert. Sometimes there is a superimposition of narrators, as in Henry James's *The Turn of the Screw*. Joseph Conrad does this regularly. In *Chance*, it makes you dizzy, you don't know where you are. If you don't pay attention reading certain Faulkner novels, like the Snopes trilogy, you have trouble telling who is speaking. It would be a never-ending task to name all the variations imagined by novelists for the figure of the narrator, whose main function is almost always to make us believe that a fiction is the truth.

The intervention of someone who speaks in the first person singular, or even in the first person plural, can sometimes be even more surreptitious. In a work as objective as *Madame Bovary*, the first word is "we." Who doesn't remember poor Charles Bovary's arrival at school? "We were in Study Hall, when the headmaster entered, followed by a *new boy* . . . ."

But as soon as we leave the classroom, the novel begins its normal course in the third person, until the end.

Just as, at the beginning of Dostoyevsky's *The Possessed*, a novel that will be narrated most of the time in the third person, another narrator appears (he won't speak again until much later, and then only briefly): "Before describing the extraordinary events which took place so recently in our town, hitherto not remarkable for anything in particular. . . ."

This "our" acclimates the reader, making him practically a citizen of the town where the story will take place.

In an impersonal novel, sometimes a character will suddenly start to speak in the first person. You have the impression he must. And this doubtless adds a necessary touch of truth.

Memoirs and Confessions

Novels that claim to be close to autobiography, like those of Céline or Henry Miller, are often highly inventive. We have trouble believing Blaise Cendrars when he tells us, in *The Astonished Man*, about his love affair at the bottom of the Seine with the daughter of a deep sea diver. Marguerite Duras, to make a stronger impression on her readers, pretended that her Indochinese novel, *The Lover*, was about her life, whereas almost nothing in it is true.

Next to these false autobiographies are the true ones, which can be great and original literary creations. Michel Leiris's *Manhood*, to name one.

The literary monuments that come to us as "memoirs" or "confessions" have a purpose far removed from a simple life story. They touch us almost despite the author, because of something extra he says when he lets loose. Saint Augustine's goal was to edify. De Retz and Saint-Simon? Saint-Simon wanted to continue their political battles. Rousseau thought that in offering his own image, he advanced universal knowledge of humanity among his readers, even if the *Confessions* quickly turned into one last quarrel with his enemies. Likewise, in *Monsieur Nicolas*, Rétif de La Bretonne pretended to construct a work of science and unveil the human heart, whereas his delirious imagination led him to do just the opposite. In the case of these authors, private life can be found not only in the text but in the notes for scholarly editions, prepared by professors who've gone to the trouble to verify the most minute assertions, to identify the most insignificant characters, to learn the age of the writers' lovers. . . . You discover that Chateaubriand fabulates more than Casanova.

Keys

When writers confess whatever they want about themselves, the choice is theirs. But when they write about others? Do they have the right to prey upon other peoples' lives? We know the saying: "Any resemblance to persons . . . ," a statement that proves nothing and has no legal value. "All the characters in this book are completely imagined, and Yonville-l'Abbaye itself does not exist": Flaubert tells the lie without even blushing.

But today, a few kilometers down the road, signs invite tourists to visit Ry, "the land of Madame Bovary." In Ry, they eliminated the cemetery around the church but kept two tombstones, that of Delphine Delamare, with its headstone in the form of a small pyramid, and that of her husband Eugène, a public health official. The day I went on my little pilgrimage, three or four adolescents were sitting on Eugène's tomb. Since they were preventing me from reading the inscription, they got up, mumbling "you can't even have a smoke in peace anymore. . . ."

Even if we possess the keys to *Madame Bovary*—Delphine Delamare, Louise Pradier, to name only a few—it doesn't help us understand the novel. To concentrate on the sources is to misunderstand the very nature of literary creation. Unlike painters, novelists rarely aspire to create the exact portrait of this or that character. What they have in mind is a much more general subject: life. Of course they take their material where they find it. A thousand little details, borrowed from one person or another, are useful. It's a little bit like inlaid furniture. No one can resist examining *In Search of Lost Time* and many other masterpieces under a microscope, looking for the slightest resemblance to people the author might have encountered. This teaches us nothing about the genius of the writer. Marcel Proust explains this very well in *Time Regained*: "The man of letters envies the painter, he would like to take notes and make sketches, but it is disastrous for him to do so. Yet when he writes, there is not a single gesture of his characters, not a tic of behavior, not a tone of voice which has not been supplied to his imagination by his memory; beneath the name of every character of his invention he can put the names of sixty characters that he has seen, one of whom has posed for the grimaces, another for the monocle, another for the fits of temper, another for the swaggering movement of the arm, etc."

A gentleman, asked if he was the model for Albertine, replied modestly, deploying the rarefied historic past tense: "We were several." [*Nous fûmes plusieurs.*]

In fact, Proust assures us, through all these infinite details the writer "recalls only what is general." He wants to show a psychological truth, and he does it by putting one person's neck onto another person's shoulders. So what some call invasion of privacy is not committed out of malice or cruelty, but in order to find a larger truth about life beneath the particular detail.

Before Proust, George Sand claimed, "One has to have known a thousand persons in order to depict one."

According to her, "In reality, people are so illogical, so filled with contrasts and incongruities, that the portrait of a real individual would be impossible and completely untenable in a work of art.... It is therefore nonsense to believe that an author wishes to provoke love or hate for this or that person by endowing fictional creations with traits taken from life; the least difference renders them conventional characters, and I maintain that, in literature, one cannot make a credible portrayal out of a real figure without plunging into enormous difficulties and going far beyond—toward either good or evil—the faults and attributes of the human being who served as the original."

Despite everything, as Freud once said, "without a trace of unscrupulousness the job cannot be done." Writers have to choose among literary conventions, the need for discretion, concerns about protecting their models—even the most minor ones—plus the esthetic standards that tell them their novel must be one way and not another.

If we writers didn't give ourselves the right to mine our own lives and the lives of others, most of literature would not exist. Not the works of Rousseau nor Stendhal nor Flaubert nor Dostoyevsky nor Proust nor Faulkner nor Kafka....

The annoying thing is that you never know how the models are going to react. Badly, most of the time.

"I have received five formal complaints, from persons about me, who say that I have unveiled their private lives," writes Balzac. "I have very curious letters on the subject. It appears that there are as many Monsieurs de Mortsauf as there are angels at Clochegourde, and the angels are raining on me, but they are not white."

Sometimes you expect the worst, and yet they're happy. Or they don't even recognize themselves and think you've caricatured someone else. Or they aren't at all angry about what you feared, but about some other detail. Sometimes a reading turns into a drama. Take the sorrow of Robert de Montesquiou when he recognized himself in Charlus. Montesquiou was very different from Proust's baron, if only in appearance. But he was the first to understand that Proust had gotten him just right. Even if Montesquiou had always avoided scandal and ruin, he realized that by condemning Charlus to sink into the depths of abjection, humiliation, and senility, Proust reached a truth that was truer than the facts. He knew that he would henceforth be Charlus for all eternity, and you might even say that this knowledge proved fatal. He confided in a friend, "I've taken to bed, sick over the publication of the three volumes that have devastated me."

The more people talked about *In Search of Lost Time*, the more upset he became. "Will I be reduced to calling myself Monte-sproust?" he asked Madame de Clermont-Tonnerre.

The town of Guéret recognizes itself in Chaminadour and an entire city is furious with Marcel Jouhandeau.

Proust writes Gaston Gallimard: "A woman I loved thirty years ago wrote me an enraged letter telling me she is Odette and I am a monster. Letters like these (and the responses!) kill all work. Not to mention pleasure, I've given up on that a long time ago."

The greatest number of dramas are, as one might suspect, provoked by female characters. Why should their models rejoice when they recognize their image in a mirror deformed by passion and unhappy love?

That slightly indecent sport of hunting for sources has resulted in many misunderstandings. Sometimes with the result that instead of the novel copying life, life copies the novel. Naturally, no one believes it, and the novelists, not life, are accused of copying. Forgive me for citing two personal examples.

In my first novel, *Les Monstres* [The Monsters], I imagined that a reporter charged with investigating an alleged suicide epidemic among felines was forced to throw a cat out the window. Well after the novel appeared, that's exactly what was done by the photographers at a well-known weekly.

The heroine of another novel, *Le Palais d'hiver* [The Winter Palace] was named Lydia; she owned a candy shop in Pau. It so happened that during the war there was actually a pastry shop in that town called Lydia's, located on the Place Royale. Everyone thought her shop was my model, even though I was no longer living in Pau when she opened it and I knew nothing of her existence. Obviously I had a real model, not at all the Lydia of the Place Royale. It was what you might call a false key. I might add that the real model recognized herself immediately; let's just say she was furious.

There are those who recognize themselves and get mad, and those, rarer still, who are happy. There are others who think that their life and their personality ought to inspire a novel. Only no one is inspired.

Reading

Reading, as much if not even more than writing, is an act that belongs to private life. Alone with a book. Perhaps we'll recognize ourselves in the pages someone else has written. Our chaotic, poorly understood existence is suddenly comprehensible. Fiction can teach us more about ourselves than reality.

We forge a completely personal rapport with beloved writers of the past. We'll never see them but we'll cherish them, even if years, indeed centuries, separate us from them. They are closer to us than members of our family, or than people we think we love. They can become our sole consolation. Elio Vittorini says it best: "In literature's greatest moments, there has always been a Chekhov, someone who abandons the novel and all other explicit representations or interpretations of his or her era, to touch the very depths of those isolated souls, those who are defeated by their times, isolated by the disarray and the storm."

True Private Life

Certain people who readily talk about their private lives never speak about what they write. As if this were even more private than private life. The accounts we settle with ourselves on paper are the most personal of all. Real private life is in writing.

In a famous book, Virginia Woolf insists that every woman who wants to be a writer needs a room of her own. It is also true for men. Anyone who writes needs a room of their own, a place where they are alone with their writing. And, in their private life, this will be the most private place.

I've often watched authors behaving in contradictory fashion — either showing you what they're in the process of writing, or holding it close to the vest. Yet another proof, if one were needed, that the most private thing in the private lives of writers is their relationship to writing. And even if they're among those who write to "communicate," they never completely share with their entourage, with their friends, any more than with their readers.

WRITING ABOUT
LOVE, AGAIN . . .

We might add, on the subject of private life, a major paradox concerning love. Love belongs to the domain of the intimate, which doesn't prevent it from being an eternal subject of literary inspiration.

Pierre Lazareff, the famous press mogul I used to work for, said there are only two things that interest the public: animals and love affairs, preferably thwarted. I think he was right. Even if you don't agree with Denis de Rougemont's theory that love is an invention of the troubadours in the West, it remains the sustinence of our literature. Without love, our literature would soon become anemic. And this goes all the way back to Homer, since Helen provoked the Trojan War, and Odysseus wandered from Calypso to Nausicaa while Penelope waited.

Chekhov worried when he was writing "The Steppe": "A story without a woman is like an engine without steam. . . . To tell you the truth, I have a lot of women but they are neither married women nor women in love. And me without women. . . ." Once they'd gotten to the fortieth chapter of *Twenty Years After*, Alexandre Dumas and his collaborator Maquet were horrified when they realized that they hadn't planned any love interest, whereas the success of *The Three Musketeers* had depended so much on the love story of Buckingham and Anne of Austria.

I can think of only one example of a contemporary novel without women—Camus's *The Plague*. But this is because *The Plague* is partly a novel about separation. Camus wanted separation to be the main theme—separation being one of the characteristics of the war he was portraying allegorically. In his *Notebooks,* he remarked that the literature of the 1940s used and abused the myth of Eurydice. His explanation: "Never had so many lovers been separated."

There are three solitary men in the novel, accompanied only by the ghosts of unattainable love objects: Rieux, the doctor whose wife is dying on a distant shore; the reporter Rambert, trapped in the city, far from the woman he loves; and the miserable Grand, long ago abandoned by his wife. But talking about separation is another way of expressing love.

So, with a few exceptions, the main subject of the novel is love. I won't go back as far as the middle ages, to the courtly genre, which dates back to the Merovingians, with Fortunat. I'll skip forward to the seventeenth century. By then, love has been solidly established in literature. The philosopher Huet defines the novel as follows: "We esteem nothing to be properly romance but fictions of love adventures, disposed into an elegant style in prose, for the delight and instruction of the reader."

That's a definition that suits neither Stendhal nor Flaubert nor Dostoyevsky nor Proust, Joyce, Kafka or Faulkner. Nor even Madame de La Fayette.

Madame de La Fayette is suspicious of love. Love, for the author of *The Princess of Cleves*, is a peril of which you have to beware. Yet she speaks of nothing else.

Then comes the eighteenth century. Suddenly, writers seem to disdain love. Their watchword is pleasure, and nothing but.

So the novel conforms to the philosophy of the moment—the French materialism that draws from Locke's empiricism. Condillac assigns no other goal to human life but "avoiding displeasure and seeking pleasure." A pleasure that, according to the great *Encyclopedia*, "makes us happy at least as long as we taste it." The prototype for these novels, generally brief and vivid, is *Manon Lescaut*. Manon will invariably sacrifice love and security for a moment of pleasure. And pleasure is the word that appears every time she does. During an argument about love and virtue, her lover Des Grieux concludes: "Being made as we are, it is indisputable that our felicity is found in pleasure, and I challenge anyone to define it in any other way."

He points out that love is the sweetest pleasure of all.

There's one notable exception, anticipating what the novel would become a hundred years later. That's *Julie, or the New Heloise*, where the love story is characterized by lack and suffering. Jean-Jacques, who has so much trouble simply living, must sublimate a guilty love that he takes pains to reconcile with the didactic and moralistic aspect of his novel.

After a time out in the eighteenth century, with its emphasis on pleasure, love returns to literature with a vengeance. It will accompany the novel in its evolution, its metamorphoses—even when the novel changes definition and objectives, as Balzac gives way to Flaubert or the naturalists give way to Proust and the novel loses its innocence, reflecting on its own nature and its techniques and adapting new rules of the game.

Throughout these metamorphoses the fundamental paradox of the novel remains. It is a fiction, a made-up story that allows us to seek and to find the truth about people and about the world. And love is one of the essential parts of that truth.

Love is sometimes demoted to a bit part. André Malraux points out that the *The Brothers Karamazov* is neither a detective novel nor a love story, although murder and love are at its heart. Dostoyevsky's real interest is in evil. You could also say that Proust talks about Swann's love for Odette and Marcel's love for Albertine, but that the true subject of *In Seach of Lost Time* is the expression of a philosophical view of the world, an emotive experience of time and the adventure of a man in search of his vocation as a writer.

Only with the surrealists do we hear about the absolute supremacy of love. André Breton, in his peremtory way, proclaims, "Love will be. We are intent on reducing art to its simplest expression, which is love."

Despite the novel's evolution, Pierre Lazareff's theory about love affairs, preferably thwarted ones, is still applicable, and may always be. What would there be to say about love if it weren't thwarted?

But whether love is thwarted or successful, what's new about it comes from what writers do with it.

André Malraux (him again) said that Stendhal cheated by not showing us how Julien Sorel and Madame de Rênal make love. Doubtless Stendhal, whose letters and diary show that he feared neither situations nor words, was constrained by the conventions of his era, not to mention by the rigors of the courts, and preferred to let readers imagine for themselves how Julien Sorel operated and what exactly was the nature of Madame de Rênal's sexual response. Likewise Flaubert, in his drafts for *Madame Bovary*, which he calls "scenarios," doesn't hold back from writing about what he calls, crudely, "getting ass." That his novel avoided explicit sex didn't prevent him from being taken to court on charges of obscenity.

In many novels today, writers no longer write about love. Instead, they write about how love is made. And I have the impression that women writers go further with this kind of description than men. Read Annie Ernaux's *Simple Passion*, Alina Reyes's *The Butcher*, Catherine Cusset's *Jouir* [Pleasuring], Ghislaine Dunant's *L'Impudeur* [Shamelessness]. Enough is enough.

There is another way of approaching writing about love. Writing is more or less an enterprise of seduction. Seduction of the reader, of course. But also, secretly, seduction of him or of her with whom everything can begin, or with whom all other means have failed, or even with the person with whom it has ended — the lover with whom you have a score to settle.

In specific cases where you are inspired by someone specific, whether they're close or far away, there remains a problem. Which is that you never know how she, or he, will react. I said in an earlier chapter that things can turn out for the worse. How could the women who inspire female characters be satisfied by their reflections in the novel, that mirror deformed by passion and by the misery of loving? Maybe they realize that when the author wrote about the love story that once dominated his life, the true lover was not the woman he was talking about, but literature itself. Kafka has his own special way of delivering messages about love, or nonlove. Take his unfinished story, "Blumenfeld, an Elderly Bachelor." A bachelor dreams of having a dog. But numerous objections come to mind. Dogs are dirty and the bachelor is obsessively clean. Dogs carry fleas. They can get sick and the disease may or may not be contagious. In any case, it's repulsive. Then one day you grow old. You haven't had the courage to get rid of the dog in time. "Then comes the moment when one's own age peers out from the dog's oozing eyes. Then one has to cope with a half-blind, wheezing animal encased in fat, and in this way pay dearly for pleasures the dog once had given." So, no dog for him. The egotistical bachelor regrets it. The ideal would be an animal he wouldn't have to worry about, that he could kick from time to time, send off to sleep in the street, just as long as this dog remained available the minute the bachelor wanted him to come lick his hands and greet him with his barks.

This horrible story is obviously intended to show Felice Bauer that its author is unfit for marriage.

The imaginative Audiberti has given an extremely subtle example — or rather a twisted example — of the secret intentions of an author and of the way a book can transform itself into a secret love message. This is in connection with his novel, *Le Maître de Milan* [The Master of Milan]. A man tells the story of his experience with a young woman, so that her aunt will read the story and recognize her. But that's not all. Audiberti has suggested that he, the author, intended this novel to function as a message to be read by a certain person: "It could be consequently that, like the Master of Milan, I may have written this novel tongue-in-cheek for someone to whom I hoped to tell, through the considerable detour of this book, the story I couldn't risk telling out loud in a flat-footed way."

Better yet, Audiberti thinks that if the person he has in mind understands that the novel is a message, she won't read it. She won't need to, because "the content of the message lies entirely in the existence of the message."

This may be too good to be true. We know about Audiberti's extraordinarily fertile imagination.

This brings to mind an ancient but still relevant function of the love novel, which is what I call the password novel. A novel that symbolizes the feelings of two lovers and becomes a fetish, a material proof of their love. In the 1900s, when a man wanted to make a woman understand what he felt for her, he presented her with a book entitled, in all innocence, *Amitié amoureuse* [Loving Friendship]. How bizarre that there was no author's name on the cover, only three stars. (The anonymous author was Hermine Lecomte du Nouÿ, Maupassant's special someone . . .). If the lady took the bait of *Amitié amoureuse*, the novel became an eternal symbol, a secret talisman of their love. *Le Grand Meaulnes* also played this role. And when President François Mitterrand got interested in a woman, he always gave her a copy of Albert Cohen's *Belle du Seigneur*. I know this from the woman who worked in the bookstore where he used to stock up.

If our books aren't destined for immortality, at least they can become the enduring passwords, the precious relics in lovers' memories.

A HALF HOUR AT
THE DENTIST'S

My friend Georges Friedmann, the eminent sociologist, was someone I held in great esteem. But whenever we were together — on the street, in the bus, in a restaurant — as soon as the slightest thing happened, as soon as an unusual person appeared, he couldn't resist saying: "There's a short story for you!" Anyone cursed with the label "short story writer" has this problem. I swore to myself that if he said it one more time, I would never write another short story. What happened instead is that I ended up writing a short story about Georges Friedmann's innocuous tic.

In my youth there was one book that irritated me to no end, *The First Forty-Nine Stories* of Hemingway. The guy had written forty-nine short stories! I was sure I'd never get there. And lo and behold, by now I've written more than a hundred. Nothing compared to Pirandello: 237, not to mention Chekhov: 649! Yet Chekhov and Pirandello are better known for their plays than their stories. This injustice deserves to be analyzed.

Why did Stendhal claim, "When you've written a dozen of them, the reservoir is empty, there's no way to continue"?

Flannery O'Connor, invited to give a talk on the meaning of the short story at a convention of artists in Lansing, Michigan, declared, "I don't have the foggiest notion what the significance of the short story is but I accepted at once as I like to make trips by plane, etc., and I figured I had ten months to find out. . . . I think I'll tell them something very grand, such as that the short story restores the contemplative mentality, but I don't know exactly how I'll work it up."

She also said, probably attributing to an imaginary friend what she was feeling herself, "I have a friend who writes both, and she says that when she stops a novel to work on short stories, she feels as if she has just left a dark wood to be set upon by wolves."

A strict Catholic, O'Connor marveled: "I have also found that what I write is read by an audience which puts little stock in either grace or the devil."

As for myself, I'd gladly speak of grace, in the other sense of the word. Of what accounts for the fact that all her short stories succeed, when it's so easy to fail. They are models for anyone who seeks to understand this art. What is remarkable is the surprise, the original angle by which she approaches each thought, each idea. A special kind of humor — which she calls the grotesque — emerges from her unusual, paradoxical vision of life and manages to impose itself as an unassailable truth.

For her, the short story spoke to the reader by means of the senses. One must guard against abstraction. She insisted: "Now this is something that can't be learned only in the head; it has to be learned in the habits." Or again: "For the writer of fiction, everything has its testing point in the eye." And also: "The fiction writer has to realize that he can't create compassion with compassion, or emotion with emotion, or thought with thought. He has to provide all these things with a body."

Like Flannery O'Connor, Marcel Arland thought that the short story had no need for theory: "What it demands of writers is love, and it has an interior rhythm that corresponds to its own nature."

It took centuries for the word "novella" to acquire the meaning it has today. In the eighteenth century, stories in prose or verse were called *nouvelles*. In fact they were often novels and could be as long as 500 pages. The novellas of the classical period are analogous to histories, to those digressions inserted within the thick novels of the baroque period. Sometimes the word *conte* was used. We refer to Voltaire's *Romans, et contes philosophiques* [Novels and philosophical tales]. Not much of a distinction is made between *conte*, fable, and novel. Or it's made by adding an adjective: moral novella, historical novella, Spanish novella. In the nineteenth century the novella parted ways with the novel, even if it was not yet distinct from the tale.

The destiny of the novella, in the modern sense, appears to be linked to economic conditions. It really took off in certain countries and at a certain stage when there were newspapers and magazines capable of supporting it: Maupassant's France; Chekhov's Russia; Faulker, Hemingway, Fitzgerald's United States. If you write a short story in France today, you don't know what to do with it. And if, as a beginning author, you bring a collection of short stories to an editor, there's a good chance you'll get this response: "This is promising. But couldn't you give us a novel first?"

To get back to Scott Fitzgerald, he claimed he was writing his stories for money, that it was a bother, and he would have preferred spending his time on a novel. He'd write them in three days, plus a day or a day and a half for revisions, then immediately send them off. The trouble was that *The Saturday Evening Post*, the best-paying and most prosperous of the "slicks" — magazines on glossy paper — protected its high-minded public. Any talk of suicide was forbidden. The magazine would have been happy to do without the "touch of disaster" that was Fitzgerald's trademark, and keep only the glamor. It turned down a few of his best stories, in particular "Crazy Sunday," set in a Hollywood where Norma Shearer, Irving Thalberg, John Gilbert, and Marion Davies would have recognized themselves. Hearst kept a watchful eye on the submissions. Sometimes the magazine would cut passages. Scott gathered up the outtakes in his *Notebooks* under the heading B (Bright Clippings). He also had a file for "junked and dismantled stories." He claimed, though I doubt it's true, that he wrote his stories as best he could and then added defects on purpose to make them appeal to magazine readers. He said they were good enough for whiling away a dreary half hour at the dentist's office. He is at odds with Henry James, who was sure that you could both love money and have a high artistic consciousness.

When he started to decline, Scott Fitzgerald moved from *The Saturday Evening Post* to *Esquire* and was paid less and less. Zelda didn't pay much attention to her husband's literary qualities (except when she felt the need to compete with him and started to write herself), but she thought that placing a story in *The Saturday Evening Post* was the best. Toward the end of Scott's life, she suggested to him that he should start to write for the *Post* again. He responded that the new editor, Wesley W. Stout, was an ambitious young man who didn't give a hoot about style and only published stories about fishing, football, or the far west. He added, "You no longer have a chance of selling a story with an unhappy ending (in the old days many of mine *did* have unhappy endings—if you remember)."

What is the difference between a short story and a novel? The main difference lies in the experience of the author. The short story, extracted from reality, is a story with a beginning and an end that seems drawn from life (whereas in real life, most of the time you don't know exactly when a story begins and ends). You write it quickly and then you forget about it. But a novel is a companion who lives with you for months, sometimes years. And that is quite delicious.

Jean-Jacques Rousseau declared rather oddly that the short story is the Corsica of literature, since nature is its only law. Goethe defined it as "an unheard of event that has occurred." "A short story must have the precision of a bank check," claimed Isaac Babel. The same Babel wrote a short story . . . about a short story. The narrator, who was helping a wealthy woman translate Maupassant's "The Confession," ended up in her arms.

At first, probably because it was written for newspapers and magazines, the short story was neatly structured, and it ended with what the French call a *chute*, literally a "fall," a surprise ending. You often have the feeling the whole thing was written to produce the surprise, the play of the final words.

If you've been a journalist or simply traveled around in the world, the short story can be nothing more than a something seen, some spontaneous observation: Georges Friedmann wasn't completely wrong. During the Spanish Civil War, Hemingway found an old man standing all alone near a bridge, after the other inhabitants of his village had fled. From this vision he created a gripping short story. Or rather an article he wrote for a news magazine that he decided to publish as a short story instead. He kept the title: "Old Man at the Bridge."

It's the same for Maupassant, who feeds on stories that are sometimes mildly erotic, sometimes tragic and cruel, of the kind you hear on farms in Normandy. In "Pierrot," which takes place in Caux, in the Normany countryside, they used to throw the dogs into a mud quarry, a deep pit, where they would devour one another. This was a short story from 1882, before the Turkish practice, circa 1910, of collecting dogs on the streets and abandoning them on the sinister island of Oxia.

Yet we shouldn't conclude that it's easy to write a short story. As for writing a good one. . . .

If we try to better define the genre, we come up against a major obstacle: Henry James. His example is worth a long study. He classifies his works as tales, novellas, and novels, and his only criterion seems to be length. He confesses, like the painter in his story *The Real Thing*, "Combined with this was another perversity— an innate preference for the represented subject over the real one: the defect of the real one was so apt to be a lack of representation. I liked things that appeared; then one was sure. Whether they *were* or not was a subordinate and almost always a profitless question." So he does not recount the brute facts he's learned from conversations at dinner parties, which he gathers into his *Notebooks*. He supposes, he insinuates, he suggests. And he never tires of analyzing his characters' interior lives, by way of their personalities or through their dialogues. His short stories, differing little in narrative procedure from his great novels, are the opposite of what you'd expect from the genre. Which doesn't prevent him from enjoying a few unforgettable successes. (I highly recommend J.-B. Pontalis's insightful preface to the French translation of James's "The Bench of Desolation.")

Another American writer, Sherwood Anderson, elder sibling to Faulkner, Hemingway, and the "Lost Generation," was one of the first writers to save the short story from the straitjacket of the well-told tale, to liberate it. For that reason he's been compared to Chekhov. He responded by saying the comparison was natural; people eat cabbage in Ohio, just like in Russia. That was why he was designated the Chekhov of the Midwest. Chekhov, who, better than anyone, dismantled the perfectly tied-up story.

Anton Pavlovich's stories often end on a kind of musical resolution that contradicts or puts into doubt what preceded. One example: "Betrothed." A young woman from the provinces leaves her family for Moscow. But Chekhov adds, gently, "as she supposed, forever."

Or, according to Ionych, one of Chekhov's characters, "People are not stupid because they can't write novels, but because they can't conceal it when they do."

UNFINISHED

Death and frivolity condemn us never to finish. In literature, and more generally in art, what's unfinished has a strong tendency to become posthumous. When Roger Martin du Gard was writing *Le Lieutenant-Colonel de Maumort*, he watched the novel swell with endless digressions just as he was feeling his powers decline; he ended up giving in or rather rejoicing in the idea that *Maumort* would be posthumous. Is it a coincidence that he gave his hero a name that is a stuttered version of the French word *mort*— death? Martin du Gard imagined a subterfuge to make his endless novel publishable. All it would take was for the unfinished novel to be explained by the death of the character, i.e., the author: "This is a work that may conveniently be interrupted at any moment, since, according to the fiction, it's the correspondence of a seventy-year-old who might die at any moment. In whatever state I leave the manuscript, all it will take to give it a plausible ending is adding a few lines to Maumort's manuscript and an editor's note." Martin du Gard hesitated only about whether to write his novel in the form of a diary, a memoir, or letters. The device could work in each case.

Whereas Kafka left *The Castle* definitively unfinished. He compared himself to a man with a rundown house filled with memories who used it for materials to build another house — his novels. But he lacked strength as he was working, so he found himself with the first house half-demolished and the second unfinished.

A word about *In Search of Lost Time*. Part of the novel is posthumous, so it can be considered either finished or unfinished, like life itself, since we imagine that if its author had lived for another ten, twenty, or thirty years, he would have endlessly corrected, revised, expanded. The narrator of *Time Regained* says so himself: "In long books of this kind, there are parts which there has been time only to sketch, parts which, because of the very amplitude of the architect's plan, will no doubt never be completed. How many great cathedrals remain unfinished!"

The true unfinished masterpiece comes to us from Musil by way of his *Man Without Qualities*, that admirable work in progress.

Pascal Pia told me that Jacques de Lacretelle and Jean Cocteau were discussing how they were going to finish Radiguet's *Count d'Orgel's Ball* as they marched in his funeral procession.

Witold Gombrowicz's unusual personality, in combination with the quirks of history, gave birth to a book that is both finished and unfinished. While he was still a law student, he decided to write a novel with a schoolmate "for chambermaids," to make a lot of money. But "writing a bad novel is doubtless no easier than writing a good one." The idea continued to preoccupy him and then he tackled *Possessed*, a higher quality novel, which appeared in installments beginning in 1939 in two Polish dailies, *the Warsaw Red Courier* and *The Kielce-Radom Morning Express*. He used a pseudonym, Z. Niewieski. The novel was both gothic and "grotesque," as those terms were understood in Polish literature — meaning it was full of bitter irony. Then came the German invasion. The newspapers ceased publication. The Polish people, who had greater dramas to deal with, would never know how *Possessed* ended.

In 1969, the year of his death, Gombrowicz admitted that he was the author of a novel that was finally published in French, not Polish, in 1973, by the Editions Kultura — still without an ending.

Gombrowicz had been assigned to cover the maiden voyage of a shipping line between Poland and South America, and he arrived in Buenos Aires on August 21, 1939, never imagining he would stay for twenty-four years. People thought he had gone into exile without having finished the final episode of his serial novel, which he normally would have written last. But in 1986, it was discovered that an ending had in fact appeared in the *Warsaw Red Courier* in the very first days of September 1939. Which confirms what people suspected: it was a happy ending, since the two major possessed characters, Walchak and Maya, are saved from evil and are finally able to admit that they love each other.

"I climbed several peaks. From one of them, I looked down into the valley": so ends a text published by another remarkable Pole. Followed by a note in manuscript: "Count Jean Potocki had these pages printed in Petersburg in 1805, shortly before his departure for Mongolia [where he was part of a diplomatic mission to China]. He gave neither a title nor an ending, reserving the right to continue or not continue it at some future date when his imagination, to which he has given free rein in this work, might tempt him to do so."

The count returned from China and wrote the sequel to what would become *The Manuscript Found in Saragossa*. Can the actual text, written in French, translated into Polish, retranslated into

French—parts of it lost, found, pillaged, rediscovered—be considered finished? Even its structure is designed to make you spin out in an endless nightmare. It's made up of stories nested one inside the other, yet they all recount the same story of a man who falls into a bed shared by two enchanting sisters. After having tasted their delights—but was it only a dream—he wakes up in a ditch, beneath a gallows. The situation repeats itself, "as if," Roger Caillois writes, "evil mirrors reflected it over and over."

Unfinished should not be confused with abandoned—*Lucien Leuwen*, for example. Doubtless abandoned because Stendhal knew he could never publish it, at least not as long as what he called the "current experience" would last, i.e., as long as Louis-Philippe remained on the French throne and Stendhal remained a civil servant. We can question, as does Claude Roy, "our naïve desire to know how it ends": "Stendhal's intentions, however, are known to us, and clear: the hero would have ended up reunited with the heroine, the imbroglio designed by Dr. Du Poirier to separate them would be foiled, and Lucien and Madame de Chasteller would be happy and have many children. Very well and good. But what also tantalizes us is not only not knowing where we would have been (we know, more or less), it's not knowing *how* the author is going to surmount the obstacles he has encountered."

In the seventeenth century, at the end of his more or less autobiographical novel, *Le page disgracié* [The disgraced page], Tristan L'Hermite declares that his hero's adventures are not finished and promises another two volumes. He died twelve years later without having written them. He would produce tragedies, poems, a pastoral novel, but nothing personal. Doubtless because in the course of his first adventures, the page, much like the author himself, took a dislike to "many diverse societies" and had only the slightest desire to live in the company of men. Melancholy, disabused, he chose silence.

By its very nature, the diary remains unfinished, since only death can interrupt the author's chitchat with herself.

"I want fame!" wrote young Marie Bashkirtseff in her *Journal.* And she hastened to add, "It is not this journal that will give it to me. This journal can only be published after my death, for I am *too naked* in it to show myself while I'm still alive."

But she kept writing in it until she had no more strength. As she lay dying, Jules Bastien-Lepage, another painter, was carried to Marie's bedside. The two of them despaired that they could no longer paint. She wrote, "Heaven have pity on us both! And to think that there are porters who enjoy robust health! Emile is an excellent brother; he carries Jules on his shoulders up and down stairs to their apartment on the third story. Dina shows equal devotion to me. For the last two days my bed has been in the *salon*; but as the room is very large, and divided by screens, sofas, and the piano, it cannot be seen. It is too much exertion for me to go up and down stairs."

Eleven days later, on October 31, 1884, she was dead.

Rousseau took notes on playing cards during his walks. On one of them you can read, "While death advances with slow steps and forestalls the progression of years, while it makes me see and feel freely its sad advances. . . ."

This unfinished sentence, holding out the promise of the second half of its rhetorical flourish, reinforces its tragic intensity. By its unfinished nature, *Reveries of the Solitary Walker* is also a diary. The tenth walk is cut short. For those who love Rousseau, it is nevertheless the most moving: "Today, Palm Sunday, it is exactly fifty years since first I met Madame de Warens."

What does Nerval mean, in his enigmatic sonnet "Artémis," which he also thought of calling "Ballet of the Hours"?

> The thirteenth returns . . . She's again the first;
> and still the only one — or the only moment:
> for are you queen, O, are you the first or the last?
> Are you king, are you the only lover or the last. . . .

Here the unfinished becomes the eternal return.

Paradoxically, Bruno Schulz's mystical vision of perfection in *Sanatorium under the Sign of the Hourglass* seems incompatible with any kind of finishing: "There are things that cannot ever be finished. They are too big and too magnificent to be contained in mere facts. They are trying to emerge, they are testing the ground of reality: can it hold them? And they quickly withdraw, afraid they will lose their integrity in an imperfect execution."

In life as in literature, certain love affairs never stop ending, fraying. Lovers promise they will conquer the obstacles, they'll be able to live together. But the deadline is constantly extended. They continue pronouncing the same phrases, making the same promises, believing in them a little less each time. Their great love becomes an empty shell.

On the other hand, some people who think they are having a brief adventure find themselves caught in the net of endless love. Thus the characters in Chekhov's "Lady with Lapdog": "Now he could see clearly that this was no short-lived affair — and it was impossible to say when it would finish. Anna Sergeyevna had become even more attached to him, she adored him and it would have been unthinkable of him to tell her that some time all of this had to come to an end. And she would not have believed him even if he had." The new life, the life as a couple they had started to long for seemed far far away, and "the most complicated and difficult part was only just beginning."

Others, more naïve, have the impression that nothing is ever over. In the amorous domain, passions are interrupted by life's tribulations. But perhaps they are only suspended. New circumstances, reunions could make things start up again. At least that's what they think.

Aren't many of us this way? We continue in our imaginations to live with the dead and with those who have left us—loving them, hating them, breaking up and reconciling with them. We take up the story the day it ended. We try to imagine what comes next. The relationship will only end when we do. It is much simpler than the memory that makes the hero of *If I forget thee, Jerusalem* (once entitled *Wild Palms*) say, "When she became not, then half of memory became not and if I become not then all of remembering will cease to be—Yes . . . between grief and nothing I will take grief."

In George du Maurier's *Peter Ibbetson*, love triumphs over separation and even death. But in the end, Peter's diary stops in the middle of a sentence: "First of all, I intend," as if the author had understood that despite all his efforts to execute his brilliant and moving fable, the universal law of the unfinished is inevitable.

Penelope and her weaving represent the unfinished at the service of the greatest fidelity in love. While Odysseus takes his time getting home, either because the gods are punishing him or for more frivolous reasons, she will undo by night what she's done by day, endlessly. But once the King of Ithaca comes home, what will become of her tapestry? It will remain unfinished, probably forever.

*

One of the Romantics' favorite themes is stillborn love, where sudden passion and separation are simultaneous, and in the space of a second, two hearts catch fire and despair. It's the ultimate sense of the unfinished. "A flash of lightning . . . then night!" Baudelaire cries out in "To a Passerby:" "You whom I would have loved. You who knew it!"

Baudelaire's passerby is in mourning, doubtless a widow, like Andromaque in "The Swan," his great poem about loss, exile, defeat—everything that interrupts the course of a life.

Before Baudelaire, a fleeting encounter with a passerby, bringing love and despair, had already appeared in Petrus Borel's tale, *Dinah, the Beautiful Jewess*.

Twice, Chekhov evokes a similar scene where a beautiful woman is sighted, only to be lost. In his story "The Beauties" which is actually autobiographical. And also in a letter to his sister, in April of 1887. He tells her how he noticed a "languorous and beautiful" woman at the window of the second floor of a train station. "My heart leapt and I continued on my way."

Anatole France speaks of "all the happy pleasures of the unfinished and the involuntary." But in literature, the champion of the unfinished is Flaubert. The constantly abortive love affairs of Emma Bovary, the great unconsummated passion of Frederic Moreau and Madame Arnoux that lasts throughout an entire life, the insatiable encyclopedic appetite of Bouvard and Pécuchet. . . .

I have a weakness for novels that end with a quiet murmur, like *Tender Is the Night*. In the last chapter, news of the hero, Dick Diver, gets more and more vague, intermittent. You learn that he set up a medical practice in Buffalo, then in Batavia in the state of New York, then in Lockport, where he had some trouble, then in Geneva, in the Finger Lakes region or "in that section of the country, in one town or another." News of Dick Diver, and the novel, stops there. Which doesn't prevent Nicole from declaring: "I loved Dick and I'll never forget him." To which her husband answers sensibly: "Of course not — why should you?"

There are punctuation marks to signal the unfinished: the three-point ellipses (in Chinese, it's six points!), but certain authors use them by the fistful, until they stop meaning anything.

The four unfinished sculptures of slaves in the Accademia in Florence have only partially emerged from their block of marble. Michelangelo chose not to fully separate them from their gangue. The spirit is not able to escape matter. Thus Elie Faure wrote: "Once he had completed half the giant, other torments, other victories, other failures demanded his attention. He rarely finished his statues, his monumental ensembles."

And a still more profound thought: "The greatness of Michaelangelo is that he understood and said that positive happiness is not accessible to us, that humanity seeks repose so that it may escape further suffering and, in order that it may not die, plunges back into suffering as soon as it has found repose."

Rodin, too, often chose to leave his sculptures unfinished, to leave room for the imagination. In the case of Leonardo da Vinci, Vasari claimed that "he would without doubt have made great progress in learning and knowledge of the sciences, had he not been so versatile and changeful, but the instability of his character caused him to undertake many things which, having commenced, he afterwards abandoned." Freud thinks that leaving things unfinished was Leonardo's primary "symptom."

Henri Michaux chose this sentence from Tsuredzure Gusa, the work by the Japanese monk Yoshida No Kaneyoshi (1283–1350) as an epigraph for *Passages*: "In the palaces of old, the requirement was that one building was always left unfinished."

In his beautiful book of interviews, *Quelque part dans l'inachevé* [Somewhere in the unfinished] — the phrase is borrowed from Rilke — Vladimir Jankélévitch responds to Béatrice Berlowitz's questions about music: "We understand why music, whose natural dimension is temporality, always expresses some greater or lesser sense of the unfinished: everything that transpires in the temporal domain, even when it's a dance or a joyous piece, distills at one moment or another a few drops of melancholy."

But if music takes place in time, "It is no less true that it renders *insensitive* the misery of temporal flow . . . Music transports and retains the musician in a sort of eternal present where death no longer matters; even better, it is a way of living the unlivable essence of eternity."

Instead of exhausting the imagination by asking why Schubert left his most famous symphony unfinished (he drafted the scherzo and orchestrated only nine measures), it would be better to ask why he chose the key of B minor, with its mood of mystery and despair. And for those who love enigmas, the *Unfinished Symphony* is less of a challenge than the symphony he is said to have composed at Gmunden-Gastein, since no one knows whether or not it actually existed.

Too great an ambition sometimes leads to a project the author cannot finish: Thomas Aquinas's *Summa Theologica*; Marx's *Das Kapital*.

Toward the end of his life, Georges Dumézil reproached himself for his lack of discipline: "My real work right now should be to concentrate on Ubykh, one of the forty languages of the Caucases." A language no longer spoken except by a single person. "It would be wise of me to abandon all the rest to concentrate on that task alone. But I lack the courage. I am not truly conscientious."

Dumézil died. The last villager too. And with him, Ubykh.

For the early psychologist Paul Janet, the feeling of not being finished is an ailment he called a feeling of incompleteness.

The artist, the creator, is not the only person struck down with the illness of the unfinished—there is also the consumer. To tell you the truth, I've never read all of Joyce's *Ulysses*, nor listened to *Pelléas and Melisande* all the way through, nor read Claudel's *The Satin Slipper* in its entirety.

My sister was twenty-one years old and she was dying. She had secrets to share and so did I. I had just written her that my marriage was falling apart. She wanted to know what I meant. But my mother or someone else was always at her bedside and we couldn't speak freely. I answered: "Nothing. I'll explain later."

But soon she began to suffer and she became delirious. She started to call for someone but I couldn't tell if it was me or someone else. Also she said: "I know for sure that I. . . ."

Even the first words of her unfinished sentence were excruciating. I often think about our interrupted dialogue, and then it occurs to me that she and I both lost the only confidant we ever needed.

Which is worse? To be unfinished or to be finished?

A strange dog starts to follow you in the mountains. Then suddenly he turns around. You no longer interest him.

DO I HAVE ANYTHING
LEFT TO SAY?

Is the final work of a writer — or for that matter of any artist — final according to the writer, or final for everyone else? Few writers have willingly put their last word to paper. Few have composed the literary equivalent of a last will and testament. And very few have proclaimed, with the poetic force of Saint-John Perse:

> Great age, here we are . . . here are the places we are leaving behind. The fruits of the soil are beneath our walls, the waters of the sky are in our cisterns, and the great porphyry millstones are resting on the sand . . .
>
> Listen, O night, in the deserted courtyards and under the lonely bridge-arches, among the hallowed ruins and the crumbing of the old termites' nests, to the great sovereign tread of the lairless soul.

Most of the time, the creator comes up dry. Joseph Conrad, who died on August 3, 1924, wrote to Gide two months earlier: "It's been almost four years since I've done anything decent. I wonder if this is the end?"

William Faulkner confessed, "I know now that I am getting toward the end, the bottom of the barrel."

There are those who have nothing left to say, but also those on whom the ax falls, who die making plans. Many were not aware that their time to live, and so to create, had expired. Tolstoy never stopped accumulating notes, projects, drafts — then suddenly he fled home to die in an out-of-the-way train station.

Johann Sebastian Bach is the exception. He sensed the end was near. So he began to work on *The Art of the Fugue*. "He didn't need it to be heard, nor played, nor even read, it was enough for him to write it," Armand Farrachi recalls in his excellent book, *Bach, dernière fugue* [Bach, last fugue]. Sometimes Bach interrupted his work long enough to compose parts of the *Mass in B Minor* or *Canonic Variations*. His unfinished *The Art of the Fugue* gives no instructions on dynamics or instrumentalization — as though such things no longer concerned him. Tchaikovsky, on the other hand, wrote to his nephew Vladimir Davydov while he was in the midst of composing his Sixth Symphony, the *Pathétique*: "You can't imagine what joy I feel at the conviction that my day is not yet done. . . ."

But nine days later — we don't know whether it was from cholera or arsenic — he was dead. If we add the emotional power of this music, which wrung tears from the composer himself, to the fact that Tchaikovsky wanted his symphony to be "a program of a kind that will remain an enigma for all," we find in the *Pathétique* everything it takes to foster legends and embody the myth of the last work.

Sometimes artists signify explicitly that a creation is their last. In the film *Limelight*, a bit of a tearjerker, Charlie Chaplin lends Shakespeare's last words to the character Calvero (a double for himself), before closing his eyes: "The heart and the mind . . . what an enigma!" (Calvero's face is covered, he is carried off. . . .) Chaplin would in fact produce two more films: *A King in New York* and *A Countess from Hong Kong*. His actual last work was supposed to be *The Freak*, the story of a young girl who grows wings — a part he intended for his daughter Victoria. But he never made the film.

Claude Roy recounted the death of Su Dongpo (1037–1101). On July 26 of his last year, the Chinese poet wrote one final poem:

I though I would end my days in this hamlet of Hainan,
But the Sky sent the Fairy to recall my soul
And I perceived from afar, very far, but for real
There where the sky is low and where the eagles fly
The earth's green head of hair
The continent at last!

On July 28, it was very hot on the boat bringing him back from exile. He turned his back to the wall of his bunk and expired.

After an operation for lung cancer gave him what he called a "permis de séjour" — a permit for living — my friend Claude Roy wrote a poem every day, a kind of exercise in survival. Did he consider these poems his last work?

For there will come a time
When everything will have been for the last time.

Molière coughed up blood and wrote a farce about a hypochondriac. He died during the third performance.

The temptation to write a book in the guise of a last will and testament can surface at any moment. "This book should be read as one might read the book of a dead man," Victor Hugo wrote in the preface to his *Contemplations*.

He announced to Jules Janin, "This book could be divided into four parts which would be entitled: My dead youth — My dead heart—My dead daughter—My dead country. Alas!" But to Paul Meurisse, he spoke of a "volume of calm verse." And to another correspondent, he confessed a concern for décor: "I am putting the last few gold stars on the rather somber sky of the *Contemplations.*"

As Kafka said, "You speak endlessly of death and you don't die." One can write what one considers a final work and then suddenly have doubts. That was the case for Gide when he finished *So Be It: or The Chips Are Down*. So he added: "No, I cannot assert that with the end of this notebook all will be finished; that all will be over. Perhaps I shall have a desire to add something. To add something or other. To make an addition. Perhaps. At the last moment, to add something . . . I am sleepy, to be sure, but I don't feel like sleeping. It strikes me that I could be even more tired. It is I don't know what hour of the night or of the morning . . . Do I still have something to say? Still something or other to say?"

He confessed, with a touch of humor: "It wasn't part of my plan to live to be this old."

What freedom in this, his last work, precisely because the author thinks it is the last? "The blank page lies in front of me. My intention is to write anything whatsoever on it." "With a dispirited pen," he skips from the memory of an accident he witnessed in his childhood, to his current anorexia (physiological and intellectual), to Ida Rubinstein, Stravinsky, Copeau, and André Barsacq, and from there to Péguy, to his journey to the Congo, to Oscar Wilde, Charles du Bos, Suarès. . . . He accumulates anecdotes and even funny stories, jokes. Memories flow without any order, gay, sad, or even tragic, such as the death of Eugène Dabit in Sevastapol during their trip to the Soviet Union. He is amused or upset and always says what he thinks.

Death is not like Tribulat Bonhomet, the character in Villiers de l'Isle-Adam's famous story, who decides to kill swans in order to hear their beautiful songs. Our swan song can be sublime or cacophonic, or there can be no song at all: Death expects nothing of us. Chekhov entitled one of his one-act plays "The Swan Song" and gives this speech to an old actor: "I'm like a squeezed lemon, a cracked bottle." But we can transpose and attribute the actor's curses to a writer at the end of his tether: "Ah! I'm a foolish old man, a poor old dodderer! . . . Old age! . . . I can play the fool, and brag, and pretend to be young, but my life is really over now. . . . I have drained the bottle, only a few little drops are left at the bottom, nothing but the dregs."

Proof that the work will be the last one sometimes emerges in the course of things. In 1963, Audiberti decided to keep a diary for a year. "Getting down to work, recounting my existence for an entire year, spent like all the other years watching films, complaining about cars, inhaling the stench, the odors of the rue des Rosiers under the first star, looking for an apartment, asking Jesus Christ to explain himself once and for all, I was unaware until the month of June that I would suddenly find myself face-to-face with a parade of officiating priests, males and females in white coats who brandished snakes made of plastic and swords of various lengths, and that these surgeons and nurses were locking me into a vicious cycle with no exit in sight."

And that is how his diary of a year became his last work. Audiberti, who died in 1965, had found a title for it which, in its extreme brevity, carries a tremendous emotional charge: *Dimanche m'attend* [Sunday awaits me].

The story of Audiberti's last book is a specific case of the rather general tendency of writers to want to publish their diaries once they feel their hour approaching. I'm reminded of Roger Vrigny. After having written a dozen or more works of fiction and nonfiction, he decided to publish excerpts from his journal. There's no doubt but that a sense that his days were numbered incited him to reveal the secrets he called *Instants dérobés* [Stolen moments].

Rereading his "stolen moments," I came across one page that tugged at my heart. He writes about "all of our ways of manipulating our pain, to occupy it, to distract it—while other people haven't the slightest clue."

Marc Bernard's last books, *Tout est bien ainsi* [It's fine that way] and *Au fil des jours* [As the days go by], are essentially diaries; sometimes sad, haunted by the death of his wife Else and by his own death, which had become a foregone conclusion; sometimes gay, for life continued around him nonetheless. He wrote "without a harness, lost on the page, without knowing where it's leading me." *Au fil des jours* was published just after his death.

While the plague held sway in Venice, Titian transformed a Pietà into an *ex voto* against the epidemic, a tragic work of art where we can recognize the painter in the features of a prostrate old man looking up at the Virgin. Titian didn't have time to finish his work because the plague caught up with him. Today he has a mausoleum in the Frari church in Venice and his painting is exhibited in the Accademia museum.

That we are incapable of knowing how much time we have left inspired this thought of Bulgakov's, in *The Master and Margarita*: "Yes, man is mortal, but that's only half the trouble! The problem is that he is unexpectedly mortal, that's the trick! And in fact, he can't even say what he'll be doing tonight."

Alexandre Dumas, in the supreme moment, is supposed to have said, "I will never know how it ends." Was he talking about his novel *Le Chevalier de Sainte-Hermine*, about the *Grand dictionnaire de cuisine* [Dictionary of cuisine] that he would leave unfinished, or about something completely different?

Ludwig Wittgenstein, in the preface to the *Philosophical In-*

vestigations that would become his posthumous work, expressed regret: "I should have liked to produce a good book. This has not come about, but the time is past in which I could improve it." Vladimir Nabokov never finished his last novel, *The Original of Laura*. At first, he added a subtitle: *Dying Is fun*. But only a few drafts were ever committed to paper until his son had it published, thirty years later. On October 30, 1976, less than a year before his death, Nabokov wrote Victor Lusinchi of the *New York Times*: "in my diurnal delirium [I] kept reading it aloud to a small dream audience in a walled garden. My audience consisted of peacocks, pigeons, my long dead parents, two cypresses, several young nurses crouching around, and a family doctor so old as to be almost invisible. Perhaps because of my stumblings and fits of coughing the story of my poor Laura had less success with my listeners than it will have, I hope, with intelligent reviewers when properly published."

Those unable to see the fatal moment nearing, who can't imagine that their writing could ever be rudely interrupted, leave in the hands of the public a text, generally unfinished—i.e., a rough draft. What a mess Pascal left us with his book *Pensées*! No matter how much you twist and turn it, rearrange its parts, it isn't a posthumous work. It's just papers—notes made by someone who was planning to write an Apologia for the Christian Religion. But it isn't even a draft of that Apologia.

In his notes for *The First Man*, Camus wrote, "The book must remain unfinished."

His premature death in a car crash gave this note a tragic significance. Actually, what Camus meant was that he imagined a monument, a sort of *War and Peace*, spanning the life of an individual and the history of a century, with its upheavals, its wars—an open-ended epic. He only had time to write the beginning—not even the beginning but the draft of a beginning. And these pages, which have been read as a touching history of a childhood, have moved readers far more than his carefully composed, constructed, deliberate books. There is an even more paradoxical fact, which raises yet another question about what we must consider a last work. While Camus was writing *The Fall,* a hopeless self-castigation and a bitter settling of scores with Parisian intellectuals, he began to take notes for *The First Man,* which, on the contrary, was full of love and confidence in humankind. What was he really feeling? Did these works alternate in importance for him? We might conclude that *The First Man* had preoccupied him for years, while *The Fall* was only a parenthesis, the expression of a mood. The contradiction is perhaps only superficial. Clamence, the narrator of *The Fall,* is guilty. But Cormery, in *The First Man,* turned his back on his country, his relatives, his roots, and hated himself. . . . In both cases, the vision is pessimistic. And, in both cases, there is the theme of exile, which always haunted Camus, who felt exiled his entire life.

As he was writing Clamence's bitter soliloquy, perhaps this exiled Camus discovered some tenderness by accessing another role for the exile: remembering childhood in the country he has lost. Thus *The Fall* and *The First Man* would be two sides of the same sensibility.

While Camus wrote that *The First Man* "must remain unfinished," Scott Fitzgerald wrote to his agent when he started to work on *The Last Tycoon*: "It is a short novel, about 50,000 words long, and should take me 3 to 4 months." It wasn't short enough, since he couldn't finish it. At the time of his death, he was only on the first episode of the sixth chapter.

Some writers have experienced the disgrace of being told that they ought to consider their new work as the final one. Take Boileau's famous jab to Corneille: "after *Attila,* stop!" [*après* l'Attila, *holà!*] Which didn't prevent Corneille from going on to write

Titus and Berenice, Pulcheria, Surena. Though Boileau did wait for Corneille to die (1684) to publish his epigram (1701).

With certain authors, including some of the very greatest, we cannot speak of a last work. With them an entire life's work is constantly put back on the loom, and so is condemned to remain unfinished. Nietzsche, Proust, Musil are in this category. Nietzsche wavers between the desire to construct and a totally free form. Only death stopped Proust from pasting strips of paper onto his manuscripts and his page proofs. With Musil, we never stop digging away at the mass of unpublished pages that supplement *The Man Without Qualities*. Critics attribute his inability to finish to masochism. But is having more and more to say, trying to reach perfection, really masochistic?

Georges Bernanos couldn't see an end to *Monsieur Ouine,* and he began to believe that the book would be as posthumous as it would be unfinished. He began writing the novel in 1931 and didn't write the final sentence until 1940. In 1934 he confessed to Robert Vallery-Radot: "My famous novel is a lugubrious urinal. I've started to have enough of pissing sadly against the same wall. Will I ever finish it?" His last work is the *Dialogues of the Carmelites.* He finished in March 1948, just as he was obliged to take to his bed, three and a half months before his death.

Saint Bonaventure, the Franciscan philosopher nicknamed the Seraphic Doctor, supposedly had the unique privilege of continuing his memoirs after his death. Chateaubriand was jealous: "I don't hope for such a privilege, but I would like to resuscitate at the ghostly hour—at least to correct my page proofs."

This chimeric wish was provoked by his worries about his *Memoirs from Beyond the Tomb*. More than once, this monument, which he intended to be posthumous, was in danger of becoming anthumous. That was due to the financial problems that always plagued the viscount. He gave some readings from the *Memoirs* in February and March 1834 and accounts of those readings were published. In 1836, one can find fragments of the memoirs in his "Essay on English Literature." Yet he complained, "I prefer to speak from the bottom of my grave." In 1836 he sold the *Memoirs* to a company, which paid him, promising they would publish nothing from them until after his death. Nonetheless, he gave a new reading in 1845.

The affair took a worrisome turn in October 1844. The company sold rights to Emile de Girardin to publish excerpts from the *Memoirs* in his newspaper, *La Presse*. An unhappy Chateaubriand later wrote about seeing his *Memoirs* reduced "to bits and pieces": "No one can form an idea of what I have suffered in being compelled to mortgage my grave."

The stockholders grew impatient. The writer was living too long. Publication of the excerpts began on October 21, 1848. Chateaubriand died on July 4. He had nearly missed his mark. . . .

In my opinion, the true last work of Chateaubriand is not the monumental *Memoirs from Beyond the Tomb*, but his *Vie de Rancé* [Life of Rancé], a departure from all his previous work. "It was to obey the orders of my confessor that I wrote the story of the Abbé de Rancé. The Abbé Séguin often spoke to me about this work, for which I had a natural repugnance."

René received his instructions in the humble abode of that ancient refractory priest at 16, rue Servandoni. *Vie de Rancé* would be his last book. "My first work was finished in London in 1797, my last in Paris in 1844." There followed a rather grandiloquent speech bringing together Tacitus, Louis XVI, and Bonaparte. "What am I doing in the world?" He concluded, "I used to be able to imagine the story of Amélie; now I'm reduced to writing Rancé's story. I've changed angels with the changing years." Which doesn't prevent *Vie de Rancé* from being an admirable book whose modern style surprises us: "Madame de Montbazon went to her eternal infidelity."

Jean-Jacques Rousseau worried about the integrity of his manuscripts even more than he worried about the judgment of posterity. Fearing his enemies, he did not want to publish the *Confessions* during his lifetime, but he was afraid that distorted versions would be circulated in order to discredit him after his death. So, this man who had made a living copying musical scores now took to creating the copies himself. According to Alice Kaplan and Philippe Roussin, "He hoped to guarantee the posthumous fate of his manuscripts by asking his protégés to prepare them for publication at the proper moment, and in 1774, he made a 'Declaration regarding different reprints of his work,' anticipating and disavowing editions that would falsify, alter, disfigure, or mutilate his work." Such problems have led today's editors—including the editors of Rousseau in the series of classics called the "Bibliothèque de la Pléiade"—to take manuscript study to heart. We have moved from an era of the Work to the era of the Text. Which has encouraged the development, in France, of a school of criticism known as *génétique littéraire*—literary genetics. The last work is not designated by the author; it consists instead of a heteroclite collection of unpublished drafts and materials assembled by an editor.

Whether or not to publish a memoir or a diary after death is a choice certain authors make at the end of their lives, in the hope of having some small chance of survival. I have known writers who speak constantly about their diaries and, in my job as an editor, I have dreaded having to read them one day, suspecting that the thousands of pages would be devoid of interest.

Louis Guilloux didn't use his memoirs as a weapon, but rather as armor. Any time he didn't want to answer a question—about his trip to the Soviet Union with Gide, for example—he declared, "I'm saving it for *L'Herbe d'oubli* [Weeds of oblivion]. That was the title he had planned. The beginning of *L'Herbe d'oubli* has been found, but only the beginning.

Is Meslier's *Last Will and Testament* a last or a first work? Meslier, a humble preacher in the era of Louis XIV and Louis XV, lived quietly in a village in the Lorraine. His will was discovered after his death—a profession of atheism and revolt. Meslier recommended that nobles be hanged and strangled with the entrails of preachers. Contrary to what one might expect, his scathing attack was not ignored. A hundred or so copies circulated until the text reached Voltaire, who guaranteed its survival.

In Saint Petersburg, I saw the desk where Dostoyevsky finished writing *The Brothers Karamazov*. "I stay at my table and I write literally day and night," he declared as he was writing book XX and the epilogue. The novel was published in December 1880. He thought of a sequel, but he died on January 28. Just behind the desk there is a dark couch. Dostoyevsky died on this couch. The desk and the couch, inseparable.

Writing forces you to consider the problem of posterity, even if you don't give a damn. Stendhal's wish is well know. He saw himself winning the lottery—either around 1880, or around 1935. Scott Fitzgerald expressed his hope in a timid, modest fashion: "I am sure I am far enough ahead to have some small immortality, if I can keep well," he noted as he was working on *The Last Tycoon*, the novel he wouldn't have the chance to finish. That small immortality was granted him. I remember that Romain Gary confessed to me, in a completely objective tone, "I believe that I am one of those whose work will survive." I had the impression that before coming to this conclusion and revealing it to me, he had considered the issue dispassionately, as if he were thinking about another person. Besides which, he wasn't wrong. A quarter century after his death, his work is read and studied.

For Sartre, the last work was by definition the one he was in the process of writing, which was, by definition, better than the last one:

> I'm thinking that I would do better today and *so much* better tomorrow. Middle-aged writers don't like to be praised too earnestly for their early work; but I'm the one, I'm sure of it, who's pleased least of all by such compliments. My best book is the one I'm in the process of writing; right after it comes the last one that was published, but I'm secretly getting ready to be disgusted with it before long. If the critics should now think it's bad, they may wound me, but in six months I'll be coming round to their opinion. On one condition: however poor and worthless they consider the book, I want them to rank it above all my previous work. I'm willing to let them run down my whole output, provided they maintain the chronological hierarchy, the only one that leaves me a chance to do better tomorrow, still better the day after, and to end with a masterpiece.

Jean Rostand says the same thing: "No sooner have you published your book than all you care about is to erase it, to obliterate it with the next one."

In response to the question "What feelings does the word 'posthumous' awaken in you?" the Latin American writer Roberto Bolaño replied, "Something like a Roman gladiator. An undefeated gladiator. Or at least that is what the poor Posthumous wants to believe to give himself courage."

In my job as editor, I once had the following, pretty awful experience. A writer who knew he was dying of cancer brought me three manuscripts. When I finished reading them, he looked me straight in the eye and asked "Do we publish this one before or after my death? . . . And this one? . . . And that one?" In other words, it was up to me to decide which would be his last work.

In 1888, Herman Melville had been forgotten for a long time. He had become a customs inspector for the port of New York. Death lurked around him. His son Malcolm committed suicide at age eighteen. He started to write *Billy Budd*. Nearly a year later, as he was reading Balzac's correspondence, he came across this letter to Madame Hanska, from October 1, 1836: "You doubtless couldn't know what profound pain is in my soul, nor what dark courage accompanies my second great defeat, sustained in the thick of life . . . Having abandoned all my hopes, having abdicated everything . . . I am certain, after this result [the failure of *The Lily of the Valley*] that my work will have no buyers in France."

Melville had just finished *Billy Budd*, in 1891, when he died. "The book remained in manuscript, disdained and forgotten, until 1924," writes the great Melville critic Jean-Jacques Mayoux.

That terrible winter night when he hanged himself on the fence of the rue de la Vieille Lanterne, was Nerval thinking about his work in progress, *Aurelia*? A few pages were found in his pockets.

We might conclude by quoting Kafka again: "And yet I'm going to die. So I'm singing my finale. One man's song is a bit longer, another man's a bit shorter. But the difference is never more than a few words."

Let's give the last word to Joseph Conrad: "I was within a hair's breadth of the last opportunity for pronouncement, and I found with humiliation that probably I would have nothing to say."

TO BE LOVED

Is writing a raison d'être? It seems to me that we ought to approach the problem more modestly, more gently, by speaking rather about the need to write. Where does it come from and how does it take hold?

Our schools, our society—or at least the one that existed a few years ago, before it underwent a profound mutation, if not a collapse—have always assigned a special value to literature and to writers. This is why children found it natural—children are monkeys—to write poems just like the ones they found in their school books. Sartre described the situation in "What Is Literature?": "We were accustomed to literature long before beginning our first novel. To us it seemed natural for books to grow in a civilized society, like trees in a garden. It was because we loved Racine and Verlaine too much that when we were fourteen years old, we discovered, during the evening study period or in the great courtyard of the *lycée*, our vocation as a writer."

In *L'homme précaire et la literature* [*Precarious Man and Literature*], Malraux posits that no novelist can exist without a library. He means that you can't write if you're not imbued with what others have written before you, that every book takes into account the books that preceed it and is, in a sense, their sequel.

Valery Larbaud goes father still: "The essence of a writer's biography is in the list of books he has read."

The painter's biography is the list of paintings he has seen.

French writers always consider themselves to be continuers rather than creators. In other countries, such as the United States, the sense of creating dominates.

If there exists in us something that is trying to express itself, we still need to find a form and even a model.

Camus has described his beginnings. In the lycée, he studied the classics. He also had an uncle, a real eccentric, who worked as a butcher but who was extremely well read and got him to read Gide. Who seemed interesting and admirable to the adolescent but didn't move him. Gide's books didn't really concern him. Then one day he came across a novel by André de Richaud, *La douleur* [Sorrow]:

> I don't know André de Richaud. But I have never forgotten his admirable book, the first to speak to me of what I knew: a mother, poverty, fine evening skies. It loosened a tangle of obscure bonds within me, freed me from fetters whose hindrance I felt without being able to give them a name. I read it in one night, in the best tradition, and the next morning, armed with a strange new liberty, went hesitatingly forward into unknown territory. I had just learned that books dispensed things other than forgetfulness and entertainment. My obstinate silences, this vague but all-persuasive suffering, the strange world that surrounded me, the nobility of my family, their poverty, my secrets, all this, I realized, could be expressed! There was a deliverance, an order of truth, in which poverty, for example, suddenly took on its true face, the one I had suspected it possessed, that I somehow revered. *La douleur* gave me a glimpse of the world of creation. . . .

I'm not going to pretend that *La douleur* is a great work. The important thing is that it spoke to its young reader. It didn't need to be a masterpiece to unleash a vocation.

"Literary"

As for me, I didn't write at all when I was in grade school or in high school. And I don't remember any book that made me want to write. Actually I wasn't very good in French. Latin was my best subject. Yet my family and friends decided once and for all that I was "literary." It's strange how often we're labeled without having done anything to deserve it. It was doubtless because I read so much. I've told how my mother, worried about finding me always lying on my stomach on a rug, my nose in a book, took me to Bordeaux to consult a great medical specialist. (We lived in Pau and Bordeaux was our capital). She was afraid that so much reading would unhinge me. Even though the doctor made light of her fears, they were not entirely absurd. We know what happened to Don Quixote after reading too many tales of chivalry. My literary reputation followed me. If someone needed something written, they came to see me. I wrote the ads for the calamitous movie theater my parents bought in Pau. I wrote for the student newspaper in Clermont-Ferrand. As a soldier in Marseille, in 1940, after the retreat, I worked in the Vieux-Port, in the cafés, writing letters for prostitutes. My sergeant, a likable but overly sentimental guy, used to rely on me to seek advice for his romantic problems in the lovelorn columns of *Marie-Claire*: "My wife and daughter are in the occupied zone. I've tried every method, including begging, to convince them to join me. I finally succeeded. And now that they're here, I've lost my freedom. What now—what should I do?" After the liberation of Paris, I was sent to the upstart newspapers that people were referring to as "products of the Resistance." I became a journalist. In fact, I have always been a scribe.

Soon I found myself at *Combat*. No better way to awaken a vocation. At *Combat* everyone had written, was writing, was going to write a book. This daily paper was practically a branch of the *Nouvelle Revue Française*, the literary magazine of Gallimard. Albert Camus was the editor. But even more symbolic, the director, Pascal Pia, was an outstanding writer, who, in addition to his talent—you might even say his genius—had this rare quality: he refused to publish. He chose silence.

In order to find out if I was capable of acting like everyone else, since I had covered so many trials, I wrote a book-length essay on the workings of the judicial apparatus, published in excerpts by Sartre and Merleau-Ponty in their magazine, *Les Temps modernes*, and published as a book by Camus in his series *Espoir* [Hope]. The title of the series was the source of many jokes, since the first books were *L'Asphyxie* [Asphyxia] by Violette Leduc, *On joue perdant* [We play to win] by Colette Audry, *Le Dernier des métiers* [The last profession] by Jacques-Laurent Bost, *L'Erreur* [The error] by Jean Daniel, *Une métaphysique tragique* [A tragic metaphysics] by Émile Simon, and now my *Rôle d'accusé* [Role of the accused].

When he accepted my manuscript, Camus gave me the boilerplate contract they used in those days. You committed to ten books. With the one I'd just signed, that made eleven. I signed with a smirk, convinced I'd never write another book. Later, still in the mode of emulation, I wrote a novel, just to see if I could. Then short stories. Writing turned into a habit, if not a mania—a mania into which I sank further every day, so that now, I'm incapable of enjoying any other activity, any other distraction. To the point where I can feel guilty if I don't write. Is that a raison d'être? When things are going badly and there is nothing else, perhaps. But I'd rather say that writing has become a way of living. You might point out that at the end of the road, whether you're writing or not writing, the result is the same. Let's just say, without giving it any more importance than it deserves, that it's a distraction, in Pascal's sense of the term.

In *The Seagull*, the famous author Trigorin pretends to complain, "I've barely finished one story, when already for some reason I have to write another, then a third, after the third a fourth. . . . I write nonstop, like an express train, and I can't help it."

The Need to Write

A publishing house like Gallimard receives close to ten thousand manuscripts a year. Which tells you how many human beings feel the need to write. What are their reasons? I've just given mine, though I'm not sure how pertinent they are. When they were young, Louis Aragon, André Breton, and Philippe Soupault couldn't resist conducting a survey entitled "Why do you write?" in a 1921 issue of their magazine, which they had baptized, somewhat ironically, *Littérature*. The answers were provocative, banal, or devoid of meaning.

J.-B. Pontalis, in a more serious interview with the magazine *Les moments littéraires*, listed the principal motivations: "to be loved, according to Freud; to have success with women, according to Maupassant; out of weakness, for Valéry—but that's not very credible. There's the decisive response by Samuel Beckett: 'bon qu'à ça' . . . good for nothing but that."

Montaigne argues that what drew him to write was solitude: "It was a melancholy humor, and consequently a humor most hostile to my natural disposition, produced by the gloom of the solitude into which I had cast myself some years earlier, that first put into my head this daydream of meddling with writing."

Lorand Gaspar admits that "there seem to be people who write for themselves at first, because it enables them to breathe better."

Kafka also had a quasi-physiological need: "When it became clear in my organism that writing was the most productive direction for my being to take, everything rushed in that direction and left empty all those abilities which were directed towards the joys of sex, eating, drinking, philosophical reflection, and above all music. I atrophied in all these directions."

For Faulkner, writing presented itself as an inexplicable necessity, beyond discussion: "The first thing, the writer's got to be demon-driven. He's got to have to write, he don't know why, and sometimes he will wish that he didn't have to, but he does."

The same Faulkner, who hated interviews, is said to have responded to a journalist with a quip whose exact source has disappeared into legend: "Well, son, I can't drink all the time, I can't eat all the time, and I can't fuck all the time. What else is there to do?"[14]

And Sartre: "I have to write. I wrote to say I'll write no more."

For Louis Guilloux, "we all write on the walls of our prison."

In other words, every human being is locked in his or her solitude. It's as if writing were the only escape. Of course, one can also write out of a desire to be alone, to enjoy one's own company, faced with a sheet of paper. But more often one writes because one is too alone.

There are those who write by imitation. Those who want to bear witness. Those who feel the need to communicate. Those who need to proclaim the truth, their truth, and those who need

14. A polite version of the same sentiment appears in Jean Stein's 1956 interview with Faulkner in *The Paris Review* 12: 28–52.

to invent lies. Those who write like a medium in a trance. In *A Life of One's Own*, the psychoanalyst Marion Milner claims a bit naively that she writes about her life to know if she can find any rules about the conditions in which happiness occurs.

In his speech at Stockholm, in 2006, the Nobel Prize winner Orhan Pamuk surveyed the question: "I write because I have an innate need to write! I write because I can't do normal work like other people. I write because I want to read books like the ones I write. I write because I am angry at all of you, angry at everyone. I write because I love sitting in a room all day writing. I write because I can only partake in real life by changing it. I write because I want others, all of us, the whole world, to know what sort of life we lived, and continue to live, in Istanbul, in Turkey. I write because I love the smell of paper, pen, and ink. I write because I believe in literature, in the art of the novel, more than I believe in anything else. I write because it is a habit, a passion. I write because I am afraid of being forgotten. I write because I like the glory and interest that writing brings. I write to be alone."

Only the irascible Thomas Bernhard rebels against the need to write. In 1963, he had just published *Frost*. Faced with the avalanche of critiques, good and bad, he couldn't stand it anymore: "I thought I would choke on the error of believing that literature was my hope. I didn't want anything more to do with literature. It hadn't brought me happiness, it had trampled me down into that stifling, stinking pit from which there is no escape. . . ."

He took a job on the spot as a truck driver in Vienna, delivering beer. Incorrigible Thomas Bernhard, who turned his rage into humor.

Jean Paulhan remarked that "Victor Hugo thought of himself as a pope, Lamartine a statesman, and Barrès a general." Once in a while, a written work actually does change the course of history. Primo Levi's example is Hitler, who wasn't satisfied with writing *Mein Kampf,* but wanted to go beyond words, to make the world exactly as he had imagined it in his book. All he did was destroy it.

My idea about this issue is somewhat different. I think that the great political personalities who maneuvered to the point of leaving a trace in history are failed men of letters. Consider the author of *Supper at Beaucaire* and the author of *Seeds of Discord.*[15]

Certain people, as Daniel Pennac puts it, don't write to write, but to have written. To pose as writers. That can explain the strange behavior of people who hire ghostwriters in order to attain the status of writer. It's also why men who have succeeded brilliantly in politics, in science, in business, go to a lot of trouble to obtain another kind of consecration, by writing a novel. Literature may have lost status, but for them it remains the supreme value.

In *The Seagull,* mentioned earlier, one of the characters admits: "It would be nice to be even a second-rate author, when all's said and done."

Panaït Istrati, the Romanian vagabond who wrote in French and whose stories had considerable success between the wars, had a point of view you can only admire. He thought that he still had a certain number of books to write. Once they were written, he planned to become a vagabond again: "Thus I would have furnished my most beautiful example: give the best of oneself, without making it a habit or a profession."

Illness and his premature death in 1935, at age fifty, prevented us from knowing whether he would have fulfilled this beautiful ambition.

15. Napoleon and de Gaulle, respectively.

Lacking Religion

Some people write because to them writing is the only thing that matters: Henry James, for example. Scott Fitzgerald thought that since James was the greatest writer of his time, he was also the greatest man of his time. (He found this idea in Ford Maddox Ford.) At the end of his life, when he was forgotten and couldn't write anymore, he always introduced himself with these words: "I am Scott Fitzgerald, the writer."

Robert Musil affirms forcefully: "I consider it more important to write a book than to govern an empire. And more difficult as well."

Pierre Louÿs had such a lofty view of literature that the idea of writing a book on commission, or even worse for money, horrified him. His attitude led to literary impotence. He who had always adored women started to ignore them and live as a recluse. Reduced to poverty, he spent his nights reading, studying, and attempting to write. The women in his life — his wife Louise, who divorced him, Marie de Régnier (Louise's sister), whom he had adored, not to mention Zohra ben Brahim, the irresistible Berber beauty — didn't understand that literature had become his true spouse.

Jean Paulhan goes further still: "What do I think of literature? Basically this: we're on earth to understand the essential, to save ourselves. Thus literature, in the absence of religion, remains in my opinion the only path . . . (But this argument demands much more precision)."

This is also Katherine Mansfield's opinion: literature "takes the place of religion — it is my religion — of people — I create my people: of 'life' — it *is* Life. The temptation is to kneel before it, to adore, to prostrate myself, to stay too long in a state of ecstasy before the *idea* of it." A feeling shared by Joseph Conrad when he writes, "I don't want to talk disrespectfully of any pages of mine."

Sartre echoes them in *The Words*: "I had found my religion: nothing seemed to me more important than a book. I regarded the library as a temple."

Even before the Romantics, Victor Hugo saw himself as a priest. And Mallarmé decreed: "This world is made to end up as a beautiful book."

Roger Vrigny wondered how others, people who don't write, could live: "I was almost ready to believe that they weren't really alive. The same kind of vertigo as if I'd been told: God doesn't exist and so, the world becomes very small. Writing was God. If literature didn't exist, the earth would become tiny, like a stone."

Literature and religion are certainly connected, for many see in writing a creation, that is, a way to survive, a promise of eternity. Yet placing hope in survival through literature seems as dangerous a bet as recourse to religion. Compared to the few writers who remain in our memory and in our affections, how many have disappeared as if they had never written a line! This is the most likely fate. Paper turns to dust. Nowadays, oblivion comes faster and faster. We used to talk about a purgatory where writers would live after their deaths. The word purgatory signifies oblivion, a provisional disaffection, but also the promise of some day leaving the shadows. Which is only very rarely the case today.

It remains true that for certain people, there is consolation in thinking that after death, they will obtain some kind of revenge. Having come to the end of the line, Scott Fitzgerald writes as he is taking notes for *The Last Tycoon* that his death will keep him from finishing: "I don't want to be as intelligible to my contemporaries as Ernest, who, as Gertrude Stein said, is bound for the museums. I am sure I am far enough ahead to have some small immortality if I can keep well."

Albertine Sarrazin, whose life and career were so ephemeral, declared that her first motivation was the thought that, if she died, people would continue asking for her books at the bookstore. She died very young, and who today goes to a bookstore to buy *The Runaway* or *Astragale*? Poor Albertine, whose lot was to die, and to die completely — like the rest of us.

Since there is little or no chance that literary work will survive, one is forced to conclude that writing or not writing makes very little difference. One can do what one wants with one's life, since, in the end, without exception, we all fall into the same void. For Camus, "Creating or not creating changes nothing. The absurd creator does not prize his work. He could repudiate it. He does sometimes repudiate it. An Abyssinia suffices for this. . . ."

Abyssinia leads of course to Rimbaud, but I suspect that Camus was thinking of a man I also knew very well, someone we loved. Pascal Pia chose silence. But if he refused to write, or at least to publish, literature was nonetheless what connected him to life. All he needed to do was to recite a few verses by his friend Fernand Fleuret, and he would say, like the poet Rutebeuf: "These are my fêtes."

Among those who are driven to write are numerous men and women who are dissatisfied with life. You drown your sorrow in the inkwell.

Literature is a compensatory activity. Pavese said, "Literature is a defense against the attacks of life."

Writing soothes the rest. What rest? The rest.

Freud too thought that literature, and art more generally, were compensatory activities. They are the expression of a desire that renounces satisfaction in reality. Art substitutes an illusory object for the real object that the artist is incapable of obtaining.

Empress Elisabeth of Austria wasn't satisfied carting her melancholy around the world. The only time Sisi approached her dream was when she wrote poems imitating Heine — bad poems, but no matter. In those poems she was truly herself, a frightened seagull who never found a resting place.

Despite what Camus maintained, writing can save us from the absurd. The young Flaubert, like many boys of his era, was furiously romantic. It wasn't easy reaching adolescence during the bourgeois monarchy. Flaubert cites two of his comrades. Disgusted with existence, one of them shot himself in the head, the other hanged himself with his necktie. Flaubert, equally despairing, didn't kill himself. He wrote. He confided his disgust for life, his horror of men and of the world, to paper.

Very often the writer, like one of Musil's heroes, experiences "the agony and the triumph of being misunderstood." So he loves to create characters in his own image, in a world where the vanquished and the afflicted find consolation. A world where the Uncle Vanyas, scorned by all, win our affection.

So we imagine that if someone writes it's because he or she has gone a little funny in the head. Let's just say we're all more or less abnormal. Claude Roy points out, "Literature begins in Greece with Homer, a blind man, in China with Chou Yuan, who must have been somewhat neurotic, since he committed suicide. The first very great Latin poet, Lucretius, was as anguished as the sublime and impotent Kierkegaard, as dark as the prodigious hunchback Leopardi, as despairing as the syphillitic genius Baudelaire."

The Inner Public

From the depths of his solitude, the writer cannot work unless he imagines a public — that's the paradox. This public influences not only content, but form. Sartre explains in "What Is Literature?": "One cannot write without a public and without a myth — without a *certain* public created by historical circumstances, without a *certain* myth of literature that depends to a very great extent upon the demands of the public."

Paul Valéry is more ironic: "Who would you want to entertain? Who do you want to seduce, match wits with, to make crazy with envy; whose minds do you want to render pensive and whose nights do you want to haunt? Say, Master Author, do you aim to serve Mammon, Demos, Caesar; or do you aim to serve God? Or perhaps Venus, or perhaps a little of all of them?"

Valéry himself resists being seduced by literature with this dry dismissal: "I don't like writers interfering in my affairs. . . ."

At the very minimum, one writes for an imaginary, ideal reader, a double of oneself, the person Michel de M'Uzan calls "the interior public."

To Be Loved

Sometime around 1850, according to Roland Barthes, the writer ceased bearing witness to universal truths and became an unhappy conscience. He affirms: "One writes in order to be loved." Barthes claims that "One is read without being able to be loved."

In order to be loved . . . In some instances, to be loved precisely by the very person who refuses his or her love, his or her understanding. In a book entitled *Ce qui nous revient* [What comes back to us], Jean Roudaut tests this idea out on Baudelaire and on Kafka:

> Designed to illuminate the author's most intimate relationships, the literary work is, by its very truth, condemned to fail; and the only person who will never understand the tottering sentence is the very person for whom that sentence is intended: Baude-

laire tries to convince Madame Aupick; Kafka suffers from the "false and puerile" image his mother has of him. Kafka's letter to his father, written to clarify his relations with his family and legitimate his solitary vocation as a writer, will never reach its destination; each time he reads to his parents from his work, it is a failure: my father "always listens to me with the greatest repugnance." In Chekhov's *The Seagull,* the extremely narcissistic actress Arkadina, whose son has become a writer, mostly to get her attention, utters a line that is the ultimate in cruelty: "I still haven't read anything he's written, can you believe it. I never have time."

To Publish

Let's admit for the time being that writing is a raison d'être. What you have written, your intelligence and your sensitivity, your artistic taste, will never come into existence, will not find a corpus, unless someone else, i.e., the editor, finds it worthy of being printed. That's the exception, if you think about the thousands of manuscripts that are rejected every year. Most of them are turned down with no explanation, with some computer-generated form letter—one version for a man and one for a woman, like in old ballads. Given the avalanche of manuscripts, there is no way of doing things differently. Yet you must take those manuscripts seriously, since whether they are good or bad, the author's emotional investment—not to mention the magnitude of work involved—is the same.

Consider what can happen even to writers who have already been published. I've known a few who've experienced the following catastrophe: perhaps they never had much success but they were in print, their books had a material existence; they'd gotten a few reviews, a few readers. And then, one day, their editor said, "Clearly you're not making any progress. We bet on you in the beginning, but we've lost faith. Let's stop." As though they were told there was nothing left for them to do but die. Or that they would never make love again.

We should probably take Flaubert with a grain of salt when he curses the need to publish. He writes to his friend Ernest Feydeau, on January 11, 1859: "I note with pleasure that printer's ink is beginning to stink in your nostrils. In my opinion it is one of the filthiest inventions of mankind. I resisted it until I was thirty-five, even though I began scribbling at eleven. A book is something essentially organic, a part of ourselves. We tear out a length of gut from our bellies and offer it up to the bourgeois. Drops of our heart's blood are visible in every letter we trace. But once our work is printed — goodbye! It belongs to everybody. The crowd tramples on us. It is the height of prostitution, the vilest kind. But the platitude is that it's all very fine, whereas to rent out one's ass for ten francs is an infamy. So be it! . . ."

To the same Ernest he adds on May 15, 1859, "The impatience of literary folk to see themselves in print, performed, recognized, praised, I find astonishing — like a madness. That seems to me to have no more to do with a writer's work than dominoes or politics."

Again on January 2, 1862, he confides:

I find printer's ink so putrid that it makes me recoil every time. I put Bovary to sleep for six months after I'd finished, and after I'd won my trial I would have stopped right then and there and never have published the volume if it hadn't been for my mother and Bouillhet. When one work is done, you must start dreaming about creating another. As for the one that's just been finished, I become absolutely indifferent to it, and if I show it to the public, it's out of stupidity or based on the conventional idea that *one must publish*—something I don't feel the need to do. I'm not even saying everything I think about this, for fear of sounding like a phony.

Flaubert is forgetting about his negotiations with his editor Michel Lévy and his machinations to influence Sainte-Beuve's critique of *Salammbô*.

Swift already referred to publishing as a form of prostitution: "A copy of verses kept in the cabinet and only shown to a few friends, is like a virgin much sought after and admired; but when printed and published, is like a common whore, whom anybody may purchase for half a crown."

We could meditate for a long time on Flaubert's cry of despair, as the end was approaching: "I am going to die and Bovary, that slut, will live!"

The Diary

Sometimes writers need to unburden themselves immediately: enter the diary. We need to distinguish between diaries an author plans to publish, whether pre- or posthumously, and diaries they keep only for themselves, although we might ask if this is ever really the case.

Sometimes it seems as if the writer leaves behind a diary to correct or even contradict his or her image. George Duhamel, a kind man without a mean bone in his body, left absolutely cruel pages where he massacred his colleague Jules Romains, among others. Reading Raymond Queneau's diary, we discovered that he was religious—even a bigot. No one could have imagined that after wishing you a good evening at Gallimard, he went over to

Saint-Thomas-d'Aquin to light candles. No one even knew that he was the kind of man who kept a diary. One day a friend started talking about diaries and Queneau noted with satisfaction in his that the friend didn't suspect he was keeping one.

People who have the diary habit bother me. I'm always afraid I'll find something I said in their next volume. This has happened to me. And once it does I'm afraid to say anything in their presence.

I knew a delightful man, Jean Denoël. He was friends with Gide, Cocteau, Max Jacob, Florence Gould, and many others. A modest person who wrote neither novels nor poems. But he often spoke to me about his diary. "I've taken precautions," he assured me. "We'll see what we'll see." Then he died. His diary was never found. I don't think that anyone stole it. He must have invented it to give himself stature — dare I say, reality.

Anyone interested in diaries should familiarize themselves with the research and writings of Philippe Lejeune, especially his book *"Dear Diary—"*.

Often keeping a diary is the manifestation of a desire to survive. This presumes a lot. What about the men or women who think the letters they've written deserve to be published and read by future generations? I've known some of them.

A Substitute for Death

Looking to literature to reach what is deepest in oneself, to discover the meaning of life, comes in large part from the evolution of the novel in modern times, at least since Balzac. By the time you get to Proust, it's no exaggeration to say that the novel has replaced the idea of eternity. The novel aims to fix a destiny. Which is why the critic René-Marie Albérès could write, "The novel is a substitute for death." But the novel doesn't succeed by capturing or fixing reality or its equivalent through the accuracy of its copy—i.e., by realism. Its truth is in style, in emotion, in movement. Emotion is what counts. Even if Chekhov maintains that "you should only sit down to write when you feel as cold as ice."

The Best Remedy

Writing presupposes an effort. It's work. Why hold yourself to it when it would be much more natural to do nothing? Writing, it seems, is both tiring and pleasurable. Much more than pleasurable. Writing may be the only possible way for a human being to tame a fundamental anguish. Gérard de Nerval wrote from early childhood. But his precocity isn't what is most remarkable. The subject of his writing is. Most of the poems he drafted were about the retreat from Russia. Why? Because his mother died in Silesia, in the winter of 1810. In his verses, the Great Army's campaigns on the Silesian plain are dominated by the image of the lost mother, who will eventually become Aurélia, Isis, Marie. These poems are also an attempt to identify with his father, who barely escaped the floods and ice of Berezina.

The Wisdom of Casanova

There are also men for whom writing was not a raison d'être during most of their lives. Then one day it became a reason to survive. Imagine Casanova in 1790, at the age of sixty-five, reduced to working as a librarian for the Count of Waldstein, i.e., as a servant. He expects nothing more from life but the chance to live again by writing his memoirs: "Remembering the pleasures I enjoyed, I renew them, and I laugh at the pains which I have endured and which I no longer feel."

That is what we might call a happy disposition.

Frequently writing is driven by the memory of suffering, of past humiliations. But rarely do those memories make you laugh.

What Else to Do?

One author in particular has given a good and very thorough explanation of how he became a writer and the place writing held in his life: Jean-Paul Sartre, in *The Words*.

Sartre says that when he started writing as a child, he was a copycat; he mimicked what he had read. Since he read adventure stories by Dumas and Zevaco, he wanted to be a hero. He wanted to be Pardaillan. At age nine he discovered that he was misshapen, sickly. He wasn't going to be a hero. He would be a saint instead. A saint? No, a writer — a writer who doesn't write to find readers, but to save humanity. He has a heart-to-heart with the Holy Ghost, in a dialogue that sounds like one of those old television commercials for Panzani pasta:[16]

> "You'll write," he said to me.
> I wrung my hands: "what is there about me, Lord, that has made
>   you choose me?"
> "Nothing in particular."
> "Then why me?"
> "For no reason."

16. In a series of television commercials in the 1970s, 80s, and 90s, the Italian village priest Don Patillo (inspired by the popular Don Camillo stories and films), appears before God to defend his love for Panzani brand pasta.

"Do I at least have an aptitude for writing?"

"Not at all. Do you think that the great works are born of flowing pens?"

"Lord, since I'm such a nonentity, how could I write a book?"

"By buckling down to it."

"Does that mean anyone can write?"

"Anyone. But you're the one I've chosen."

Then the young Sartre discovers the existence of death: vertigo and terror. But he reflects. Death is a transition, necessary for a gift to be realized, for a man to be reborn, transformed into a book: "Viewed from the height of my tomb, my birth appeared to me as a necessary evil, as a quite provisional embodiment that prepared for my transfiguration: in order to be reborn, I had to write."

He compares himself to a chrysalis. The day it bursts open, butterflies escape and land on the shelves of National Library. Those butterflies are books, of course, flapping their thousands of pages. Suddenly, he believes he's destined to live to a ripe old age. The Holy Ghost has ordered a long and exacting literary task. He won't let him die before he's carried it out. His friends, his comrades savor life because they know that at any moment, an accident or an illness can cut the thread. With Sartre, whose destiny is set, it's as if he were already dead, that is, inducted into immortality.

"I chose as my future the past of a great immortal and I tried to live backwards. Between the age of nine and ten, I became completely posthumous."

In the end, Sartre describes his literary vocation as a tracing paper version of religion. Having recovered from his childhood fantasies, he concludes, "I've given up the office but not the frock: I still write. What else is there to do?"

"What else is there to do?" was Beckett's response, too. Asking why we need to write and knowing whether writing gives life meaning are intimidating questions (in intimidating, there is intimate). All we can do is circle round and round the question, as if we were scared of getting burned. "What else to do?": that may be the last word.

WORKS CITED

In addition to many works mentioned by Roger Grenier, we list here, chapter by chapter, readily available English translations or original English editions of works from which the author quotes.

"The Land of Poets"

Barthes, Roland. *Critical Essays*. Translated by Richard Howard. Evanston, IL: Northwestern University Press, 1972.

Baudelaire, Charles. *My Heart Laid Bare and Other Prose Writings*. Translated by Norman Cameron. New York: Haskell House Publishers, 1975.

De Quincey, Thomas. "On Murder Considered as One of the Fine Arts." *Blackwood's Magazine*, Jan–June 1827.

Dostoyevsky, Fyodor. *The Brothers Karamazov*. Translated by Richard Pevear and Larissa Volokhonsky. New York: Farrar, Straus and Giroux, 1990.

Faulkner, William. *Pylon*. New York: Random House, 1985.

Musil, Robert. *The Man Without Qualities*. Translated by Sophie Wilkins. New York: Vintage, 1996.

Proust, Marcel. "The Filial Sentiments of a Parricide," in *Marcel Proust: A Selection of His Miscellaneous Writings*. Translated by Gerard Hopkins. London: A. Wingate, 1948.

Shakespeare, William. *Macbeth*. New York: W. W. Norton, 2004.

Stendhal. *Lamiel*. Translated by T. W. Earp. New York: New Directions, 1952.

———. *The Private Diaries of Stendhal*. Translated by Robert Sage. New York: Doubleday, 1954.

Waiting and Eternity

Apollinaire, Guillaume. *Alcools*. Translated by Donald Revell. Middletown, CT: Wesleyan University Press, 1995.

Artaud, Antonin. *The Theater and Its Double*. Translated by Mary Caroline Richards. New York: Grove Press, 1958.

Baudelaire, Charles. "Dream of a Curious Character," in *The Flowers of Evil*. Translated by Keith Waldrop. Middletown, CT: Weslyan University Press, 2006.

———. "To a Woman Passing By," in *The Flowers of Evil*.

Beckett, Samuel. *Happy Days*. New York: Grove Press, 1961.

Blanchot, Maurice. *Awaiting Oblivion*. Translated by John Gregg. Lincoln, NE: University of Nebraska Press, 1999.

Camus, Albert. *The Stranger*. Translated by Matthew Ward. New York: Vintage, 1989.

———. "Summer in Algiers," from *Nuptials*. Collected in *Lyrical and Critical Essays*. Translated by Ellen Conroy Kennedy. New York: Vintage, 1970.

Chekhov, Anton. "A Boring Story," in *Selected Stories of Anton Chekhov*. Translated by Richard Pevear and Larissa Volokhonsky. New York: Random House, 2000.

———. *Uncle Vanya: A Comedy in Four Acts*. Translated by Jenny Covan. New York: Brentano's, 1922.

Conrad, Joseph. "To-morrow," in *Typhoon and Other Stories*. New York: Doubleday, 1921.

Deleuze, Gilles, and Leopold von Sacher-Masoch. *Masochism: Coldness and Cruelty & Venus in Furs*. Translated by Jean McNeil. New York: Zone Books, 1999.

Dostoyevsky, Fyodor. *The Idiot*. Translated by David McDuff. New York: Penguin, 2004.

Ernaux, Annie. *Simple Passion*. Translated by Tanya Leslie. New York: Seven Stories Press, 2003.

Fitzgerald, F. Scott. *The Great Gatsby*. New York: Charles Scribner's Sons, 1925.

Flaubert, Gustave. *A Sentimental Education*. Translated by Douglas Parmée. Oxford: Oxford University Press, 1989.

Gide, André. *Fruits of the Earth*. Translated by D. Bussy. New York: Penguin Modern Classics, 1970.

Homer. *The Odyssey*. Translated by Robert Fagles. New York: Penguin, 1996.

James, Henry. "The Beast in the Jungle," in *Selected Tales*. New York: Penguin, 2001.

————. "The Bench of Desolation," in *The Complete Stories of Henry James: 1898–1910*. New York: Penguin, 1999.

Mansfield, Katherine. "The Young Girl," in *The Garden Party and Other Stories*. New York: Knopf, 1922.

Pascal, Blaise. "Discourse on the Passion of Love," in *Blaise Pascal: Thoughts, Letters, and Minor Works*. Translated by O. W. Wight. New York: P.F. Collier & Son, 1910.

Woolf, Virginia. *To the Lighthouse*. Oxford: Oxford University Press, 2006.

Leave-Taking

Bataille, Georges. *The Bataille Reader*. Oxford: Blackwell Publishers, 1997.

Baudelaire, Charles. "Solitude," in *Baudelaire, His Prose and Poetry*. Translated by Joseph T. Shipley. New York: Boni and Liveright, 1919.

Beckett, Samuel. *Molloy*. New York: Grove Press, 1994.

Blanchot, Maurice. *Faux Pas*. Translated by Charlotte Mandell. Stanford, CA: Stanford University Press, 2002.

Camus, Albert. *The Myth of Sisyphus*. Translated by Justin O'Brien. New York: Vintage, 1991.

————. *The Stranger*. Translated by Matthew Ward. New York: Vintage, 1989.

Carlyle, Thomas. "Novalis." *The Foreign Review* 4.7 (1829): 97–141.

Chekhov, Anton. *Uncle Vanya: A Comedy in Four Acts*. Translated by Jenny Covan. New York: Brentano's 1922.

Conrad, Joseph. *'Twixt Land and Sea*. Cambridge: Cambridge University Press, 2008.

du Perron, Edgar. *Country of Origin*. Amherst: University of Massachusetts Press, 1984.

Flaubert, Gustave. *A Sentimental Education*. Translated by Douglas Parmée. Oxford: Oxford University Press, 1989.

————. *The Letters of Gustave Flaubert: 1857–1880*. Translated by Francis Steegmuller. Cambridge, MA: Harvard University Press, 1980.

Hemingway, Ernest. *For Whom the Bell Tolls*. New York: Simon & Schuster, 1940.

Hofmannsthal, Hugo von. "The Tale of Night Six Hundred and Seventy Two," in *The Whole Difference: Selected Writings of Hugo von Hofmannsthal*. Translated by Michael Henry Heim. Princeton, NJ: Princeton University Press, 2008.

Lajolo, Davide. *An Absurd Vice: A Biography of Ceasar Pavese*. Translated by Mario and Mark Pietralunga. New York: New Directions, 1983.

Leiris, Michel. *Aurora*. Translated by Anna Warby. London: BCM Atlas Press, 1990.

Malraux, André. *La voie royale* [The Way of the Kings]. Paris: Grasset, 1996.

Malraux, André. *Lazarus*. Translated by Terence Kilmartin. London: Macdonald and Jane's, 1977.

Melville, Herman. *Bartleby the Scrivener*. New York: Melville House, 2004.

Montaigne, Michel de. *The Complete Essays of Montaigne*. Translated by Donald M. Frame. Stanford, CA: Stanford University Press, 1958.

Pavese, Cesare. *This Business of Living*. Translated by A. E. Murch. New Brunswick, NJ: Transaction Publishers, 2009.

Poe, Edgar Allan. *Histoires Extrordinaires* [*Extraordinary Stories*]. Translated by Charles Baudelaire. Paris: Éditions Nilsson, 1929.

Private Life

Balzac, Honoré de. *The Letters of Honoré de Balzac to Madame Hanska*. Translated by Katharine Prescott Wormeley. Boston: Little, Brown and Co., 1900.

Chekov, Anton. *Notebook of Anton Chekov.* Translated by S. S. Koteliansky and Leonard Woolf. New York: Ecco Press, 1987.

Conrad, Joseph. *A Personal Record: Some Reminiscences.* New York: Cosimo Classics, 2005.

Cortázar, Julio. "A Leg of the Journey," in *Unreasonable Hours.* Translated by Alberto Manguel. Toronto: Coach House Press, 1995.

Dostoyevsky, Fyodor. *The Devils: The Possessed.* Translated by David Magarshack. New York: Penguin, 1971.

Dickens, Charles. Quoted in John Forster, *The Life of Charles Dickens.* Boston: Estes and Lauriat, 1872.

Fitzgerald, F. Scott. *The Notebooks of F. Scott Fitzgerald.* Edited by Matthew Bruccoli. New York: Harcourt Brace Jovanovich, 1978.

Flaubert, Gustave. *Madame Bovary.* Translated by Lydia Davis. New York: Penguin, 2010.

James, Henry. "The Real Right Thing," in *The Altar of the Dead, The Beast in the Jungle, The Birthplace, and Other Tales.* New York: Charles Scribner's Sons, 1909.

Nerval, Gérard de. *Daughters of Fire.* Translated by James Whitall. New York: Nicholas L. Brown, 1922.

Nietzsche, Friedrich. *Human, All Too Human: A Book for Free Spirits.* Translated by R. J. Hollingdale. Cambridge: Cambridge University Press, 1996.

O'Connor, Flannery. *Mystery and Manners: Occasional Prose.* New York: Farrar, Straus and Giroux, 1969.

Proust, Marcel. *By Way of Sainte-Beuve.* Translated by Sylvia Townsend Warner. London: Chatto & Windus, 1958.

———. *Jean Santeuil.* Translated by Gerard Hopkins. New York: Simon and Schuster, 1956.

———. *Time Regained: In Search of Lost Time, Volume VI.* Translated by Terence Kilmartin. New York: Random House, 1999.

Roubaud, Jacques. *Something Black.* Translated by Rosmarie Waldrop. Normal, IL: Dalkey Archive Press, 1990.

Sand, George. *Story of My Life: The Autobiography of George Sand.* A group translation edited by Thelma Jurgrau. Albany: State University of New York Press, 1991.

Valéry, Paul. *Introduction to the Method of Leonardo da Vinci.* Translated by Thomas MacGreevy. London: J. Rodker, 1929.

Woolf, Virginia. "A Sketch of the Past," in *Moments of Being*. New York: Harcourt, 1985.

Writing about Love, Again . . .

Breton, André. *Manifestoes of Surrealism*. Translated by Richard Seaver and Helen R. Lane. Ann Arbor, MI: University of Michigan Press, 1969.

Camus, Albert. *Notebooks: 1935–1942*. Translated by Philip Thody. Chicago: Ivan R. Dee, 2010.

Chekov, Anton. *The Life and Letters of Anton Tchekhov*. Translated by S. S. Koteliansky and Philip Tomlinson. New York: Cassell and Co., 1925.

Huet, Pierre-Daniel. *History of Romances*. Translated by Stephen Lewis. London: J. Hooke, 1715.

Kafka, Franz. "Blumenfeld, an Elderly Bachelor." Translated by Tania and James Stern. In *Kafka: The Complete Stories*. New York: Schocken Books Inc., 1995.

Prevost, Abbé. *Manon Lescaut*. Translated by Leonard Tancock. New York: Penguin Classics, 1992.

A Half Hour at the Dentist's

Fitzgerald, F. Scott. "Crazy Sunday," in *Babylon Revisited and Other Stories*. New York: Charles Scribner's Sons, 1960.

———. *The Letters of F. Scott Fitzgerald*. Edited by Andrew Turnbull. New York: Charles Scribner's Sons, 1963.

James, Henry. *The Real Thing*. New York: Macmillan, 1922.

O'Connor, Flannery. *The Habit of Being*. New York: Farrar, Straus and Giroux, 1988.

———. *Mystery and Manners*. New York: Farrar, Straus and Giroux, 1970.

Unfinished

Bashkirtseff, Marie. *Journal of Marie Bashkirtseff*. Translated by A. D. Hall and G. B. Heckel. New York: Rand McNally & Co., 1898.

Baudelaire, Charles. "To a Woman Passing By," in *The Flowers of Evil*. Translated by Keith Waldrop. Middletown, CT: Weslyan University Press, 2006.

Chekhov, Anton. *A Life in Letters*. Edited by Rosamund Bartlett. Translated by Anthony Phillips. New York, Penguin, 2004.

———. *Lady with Lapdog and Other Stories*. Translated by David Magarshack. New York: Penguin, 1995.

Faulkner, William. *The Wild Palms (If I Forget Thee, Jerusalem)*. New York: Vintage, 1995.

Faure, Elie. *History of Art*, III. Translated by Walter Pach. New York: Harper & Brothers Publishers, 1923.

Fitzgerald, F. Scott. *Tender Is the Night*. New York: Charles Scribner's Sons, 1995.

Nerval, Gérard de. "Artemis," in *Selected Writings*. Translated by Richard Sieburth. New York: Penguin, 1999.

Potocki, Jean. *The Manuscript Found in Saragossa*. Translated by Ian MacLean. New York: Penguin, 1996.

———. Cited by Roger Caillois in the preface to *The Saragossa Manuscript*. Translated by Elisabeth Abbott. New York: Orion Press, 1960.

Proust, Marcel. *Time Regained: In Search of Lost Time, Volume VI*. Translated by Terence Kilmartin. New York: Random House, 1999.

Rousseau, Jean-Jacques. "Notes for the Reveries," in *Religious, Moral, and Literary Writings*. Translated by Christopher Kelly. Lebanon, NH: University Press of New England, 2006.

———. *Reveries of the Solitary Walker*. Translated by Peter France. New York: Penguin, 1980.

Schulz, Bruno. *Sanatorium under the Sign of the Hourglass*. Translated by Celina Wieniewska. New York: Houghton Mifflin, 1997.

Vasari, Giorgio. *Lives of the Most Eminent Painters, Sculptors, and Architects*. Translated by Mrs. Jonathan Foster. London: Bell and Daldy, 1871.

Do I Have Anything Left to Say?

Balzac, Honoré de. *The Letters of Honoré de Balzac to Madame Hanska.* Translated by Katharine Prescott Wormeley. Boston: Little, Brown and Co., 1900.

Bernhard, Thomas. *My Prizes: An Accounting.* Translated by Carol Brown Janeway. New York: Knopf, 2010.

Bolaño, Roberto. Interview with Mónica Maristain for *Playboy*, Mexico Edition, July 2003. In *Roberto Bolaño: The Last Interview and Other Conversations.* Translated by Sybil Perez. Brooklyn, NY: Melville House, 2009.

Bulgakov, Mikhail. *The Master and Margarita.* Translated by Diana Burgin and Katherine Tiernan O'Connor. New York: Vintage, 1996.

Camus, Albert. "Encounters with André Gide," in *Lyrical and Critical Essays.* Translated by Ellen Conroy Kennedy. New York: Vintage, 1970.

————. *The First Man.* Translated by David Hapgood. New York: Knopf, 1994.

Chateaubriand, François-René. *Memoirs from Beyond the Tomb.* Translated by Robert Baldick. New York: Penguin, 2014.

Chekhov, Anton. *The Seagull.* Translated by Laurence Senelick. New York: W. W. Norton, 2010.

Chekhov, Anton. "The Swan Song," in *The Plays of Anton Chekhov.* Translated by Marian Fell. New York: Charles Scribner's Sons, 1916.

Conrad, Joseph. *Tales of Unrest.* New York: Doubleday, 1925.

————. *Heart of Darkness.* New York: Penguin, 2007.

Faulkner, William. William Faulkner to Joan Williams. In *Selected Letters.* Edited by Joseph Blotner. New York: Vintage, 1978.

Gide, André. *So Be It: or, The Chips Are Down.* Translated by Justin O'Brien. New York: Knopf, 1959.

Grove, Sir George, ed. *Grove's Dictionary of Music and Musicians.* New York: Macmillan, 1911.

Gwynn, Frederick L., and Joseph L. Blotner, eds. *Faulkner in the University.* Charlottesville: The University Press of Virginia, 1995.

Kafka, Franz. *Diaries 1910–1923.* Translated by Joseph Kresh and Martin Greenburg. New York: Schocken Books, Inc. 1976.

Kaplan, Alice, and Philippe Roussin. "A Changing Idea of Literature: The Bibliothèque de la Pléiade." *Yale French Studies* 89 (1996): 254.

Mayoux, Jean-Jacques. *Melville.* Translated by John Ashberry. New York: Grove Press, 1960.

Montaigne, Michel de. *The Complete Essays.* Translated by Donald M. Frame. Stanford, CA: Stanford University Press, 1958.

Nabokov, Vladimir. *Nabokov's Butterflies: Unpublished and Uncollected Writings.* Boston: Beacon Press, 2000.

Perse, Saint-John. "Chronicle," in *An Introduction to French Poetry.* Translated by Stanley Appelbaum. New York: Dover Publications, 1969.

Sartre, Jean Paul. *The Words.* Translated by Bernard Frechtman. New York: Vintage, 1981.

Wittgenstein, Ludwig. Preface to *Philosophical Investigations.* Translated by G. E. M. Anscombe, P. M. S. Hacker, and Joachim Schulte. London: Wiley-Blackwell, 2009.

To Be Loved

Barthes, Roland. *Critical Essays.* Translated by Richard Howard. Evanston, IL: Northwestern University Press, 1972.

Bernhard, Thomas. *My Prizes: An Accounting.* Translated by Carol Brown Janeway. New York: Knopf, 2010.

Camus, Albert. "Encounters with André Gide," in *Lyrical and Critical Essays.* Translated by Ellen Conroy Kennedy. New York: Knopf, 1970.

———. *The Myth of Sisyphus.* Translated by Justin O'Brien. New York: Vintage, 1991.

Casanova, Giacomo. *History of My Life.* Translated by Willard R. Trask. Baltimore: Johns Hopkins University Press, 1997.

Chekhov, Anton. *The Seagull.* Translated by Laurence Senelick. New York: W. W. Norton, 2010.

Conrad, Joseph. *Tales of Unrest.* New York: Doubleday, 1925.

Faulkner, William. *Faulkner in the University* [interviews]. Edited by Frederick L. Gwynn and Joseph L. Blotner. Charlottesville, VA: The University Press of Virginia, 1995.

Flaubert, Gustave. *The Letters of Gustave Flaubert: 1857–1880*. Translated by Francis Steegmuller. Cambridge, MA: Harvard University Press, 1980.

Kafka, Franz. *Diaries, 1910–1923*. Translated by Joseph Kresh and Martin Greenburg. New York: Schocken Books, 1976.

Mansfield, Katherine. *Journal of Katherine Mansfield*. London: Constable, 1954.

Pamuk, Orhan. "My Father's Suitcase," Translated by Maureen Freely. Nobel lecture presented 6 December 2006. http://www.nobelprize .org/nobel_prizes/literature/laureates/2006/pamuk-lecture_en .html.

Paulhan, Jean. *The Flowers of Tarbes: Or, Terror in Literature*. Translated by Michael Syrontinski. Champaign, IL: University of Illinois Press, 2006.

Pavese, Cesare. *This Business of Living*. Translated by A. E. Murch. New Brunswick, NJ: Transaction Publishers, 2009.

Sartre, Jean-Paul. *"What Is Literature?" and Other Essays*. Translated by Bernard Frechtman. Cambridge, MA: Harvard University Press, 1988.

———. *The Words*. Translated by Bernard Frechtman. New York: Vintage, 1981.

Swift, Jonathan. "Thoughts on Various Subjects, Moral and Diverting," in *The Works of the Reverend Jonathan Swift*. New York: William Durell and Co., 1812.

Valéry, Paul. *Cahiers/Notebooks, Volume 2*. Translated by Rachel Killick, Pobert Pickering, Norma Rinsler, Stephen Romer, and Brian Stimpson. New York: Peter Lang, 2000.